The ALLURE of
Celebrity Dating

SAFAREE SAMUELS
with JASON GATHING

Contents

Introduction

Get ready to dive headfirst into the intoxicating world of celebrity dating! In *The Allure of Celebrity Dating*, we're about to embark on an exhilarating journey that delves deep into the mesmerizing tapestry of love and fame, unraveling the irresistible allure that envelops them both. Brace yourself for a whirlwind exploration of the lives of those who flourish under the unrelenting spotlight of public attention. We'll unearth the electrifying highs and nerve-racking lows of romance in a realm where privacy is a precious rarity and the scrutiny of the media never relents. It's a ride you won't want to miss!

Within the pages of this mesmerizing book, you'll be introduced to stories of A-list affairs that sparkle on the red carpet but conceal tantalizing secrets behind the scenes. We'll reveal the passionate world of love on set, where on-screen chemistry often overflows into real life, blurring the line between reality and fantasy.

In a realm where paparazzi lenses never stop clicking, and where rumors and scandals can shake the very foundations of a relationship, we'll navigate the intricate journey of enduring love. From concealed rendezvous in hidden corners to the intense scrutiny of relationships in the digital age, each chapter offers a thrilling glimpse into the diverse universe of celebrity romance.

But amid the shimmering glamour, we'll also lay bare the genuine stories of heartbreak and the second chances that follow. We'll delve into the world of relationships between celebrities and everyday people, where authentic connections are nurtured beyond the glitz of stardom.

As we journey through the intriguing landscape of celebrity dating, we'll gather invaluable lessons from those who've walked this exciting path. Celebrities will generously share their insight, offering you priceless advice on navigating the tumultuous waters of love, fame, and the eternal quest for privacy.

Last, we'll turn our gaze toward the thrilling unknown, speculating on the evolving dynamics in celebrity dating and pondering what the future holds for the next generation of stars and their romances.

With every page you turn, you'll be drawn deeper into the intoxicating world of celebrity dating. You'll unearth hidden truths, delve into untold stories, and embark on a quest to fathom the essence of human connection in the most extraordinary of circumstances.

So, dear reader, fasten your seatbelt and prepare for an exciting adventure. As we journey through the captivating universe of celebrity dating, may you discover inspiration and insight that will leave your heart racing and your spirit electrified.

CHAPTER ONE

Relationship Unfolding

It all started when two celebrities forged an extraordinary love story that defied the odds. Through the whirlwind of stardom, they became each other's unwavering support system. Their relationship was a subject of constant speculation, yet the starlet in the alliance refused to officially confirm it.

In the vibrant core of the concrete jungle, the two aspiring artists bonded over a shared passion for music. The moment they crossed paths, their connection was electrifying. Together, they invested their all in the relationship, forming a profound and unbreakable bond capable of withstanding any challenge. In the unspoken dynamics, the significant role he played in shaping her beats became evident over time. It wasn't until the later stages that it was articulated – he was the architect contributing to designing the masterpiece we witness each day.

However, fame was a fickle companion, and it didn't always smile upon them. "The allure of the industry makes you prioritize material things, causing you to forget about the essence of old-fashioned love," she stated, as her eyes reflected the longing in her heart. Regarding his role in the situation, the notion that most women wouldn't desire for their partner to be in the spotlight, drawing attention from numerous admirers, adds complexity. He grappled with the concept that she desired to have her cake and eat it too – aspiring for the superstar lifestyle while ensuring the peace of mind of having someone safe at home.

As her career continued to skyrocket, they wrestled with the distinct challenges of living under the spotlight. As the situation took an unexpected twist, he, feeling a sense of amusement while his trust wavered, discreetly advised, "If there's any questionable business, it's better for it to unfold discreetly behind the scenes than right before your eyes," delving into the intricacies of their relationship. In a moment of introspection, one thought out loud, acknowledging that if their passion had led them in a different direction, their fairytale might have taken a different course, expressing a reason for the shady undertaking.

Finally, enough was enough. They reached a crucial point where a tough decision had to be made. They decided to put aside their future plans temporarily and focus on the present. They acknowledged that the challenges of the industry are unpredictable. As fame's pressures increased, their love faded, becoming more distant each day. Feeling the weight of the situation, he reflected on her business travels and discreet conversations in high-class private industry rooms. He knew their relationship was at a point of no return for the time being.

And so their extraordinary love story, filled with highs and lows, ended like a melody in the world of fame, reminding us that true love is a rare and delicate gem.

Despite the enticing allure of success, the industry's darker side can undermine the most cherished relationships.

CHAPTER TWO

Behind The Spotlight

In the vast landscape of fame and fortune, there exists a world where love intertwines with stardom, captivating the collective imagination of the masses. Therein lies the realm of celebrity dating: a place where the ordinary rules of romance seem suspended, and the extraordinary takes center stage. But what is it about the premise of celebrity dating that holds such immense appeal?

The allure is undeniable. From the outside looking in, it appears to be a whirlwind of glamorous outings, extravagant gifts, and breathtaking vacations. The world watches with eager anticipation as two famous individuals come together, their lives entwined in a dance of luxury and grandeur. It is a spectacle, a window into a world that many can only dream about.

Part of the appeal lies in the fantasy that dating a celebrity can fulfill. It is a chance to escape the mundane and embrace a life that is larger than life itself. Being swept off one's feet by a charismatic star, walking hand in hand on red carpets, and basking in the glow of adoring fans holds an undeniable, allure feeds into our desire for excitement, adventure, and a taste of the extraordinary.

Dating within the celebrity realm offers a unique bond that transcends the ordinary. Celebrities understand the pressures and challenges that come with fame. They navigate a world constantly scrutinized, where every move is dissected by the media and fans. In each other, they find solace and understanding, a shared experience that forms a deep connection. A sense of camaraderie comes from knowing someone understands the highs and lows of their extraordinary lives.

Yet, for all its glitz and glamour, dating within the celebrity realm is not without its challenges. Privacy becomes a scarce commodity, as the world watches and dissects every aspect of the relationship. What may seem like a fairytale romance can quickly turn into a media frenzy, where tabloids paint narratives and speculation runs rampant. The pressure to maintain a flawless image and keep up appearances can strain even the strongest of connections.

However, beneath the surface, genuine connections transcend the spotlight. Amidst the chaos, true love can blossom. Celebrity relationships built on trust, mutual respect, and shared values have stood the test of time. They offer a beacon of hope amidst the sea of superficiality, reminding us that love can flourish even in the most extraordinary circumstances.

Exploring the appeal of dating within the celebrity realm is a journey that uncovers both the enchantment and the complexities unknown at the start of a relationship. Exploring the appeal invites us to examine our own fascination with fame and love, to question our perceptions of what defines a successful relationship. Exploring the appeal challenges us to see beyond the glitz and glamour to recognize the humanity that exists within every celebrity.

The appeal of dating within the celebrity realm reflects our innate desire for connection, excitement, and a taste of the extraordinary. Celebrity dating invites us to dream, to wonder, and to indulge in the fantasy that love, even in stardom, can transcend the ordinary and bring forth something extraordinary.

CHAPTER THREE

A-list Affairs (Stories of High-Profile Romance)

Being in the public eye carries an undeniable allure, an intoxicating mix of excitement and perks that few can experience. It is a world where fame opens doors to extraordinary opportunities, where every step is followed by adoring fans, and where the spotlight shines brightly on every part of one's life. The excitement that comes with being in the public eye is like a constant surge of energy, fueling the dreams and aspirations of those who bask in its glow. One of the most exhilarating parts of being in the public eye is the sense of validation it brings. To have one's talent, hard work, or unique qualities recognized and celebrated on a grand scale is an affirmation like no other. It is a validation of one's worth, a testament to the dedication and sacrifices made to achieve success.

The adoration and support from fans further amplify this sense of validation, as their admiration becomes a driving force that propels individuals to reach new heights. Once this status is achieved, the perks of being in the public eye are abundant and often luxurious. From glamorous red-carpet events and VIP treatment at high-end establishments to exclusive parties and lavish gifts, the world becomes a playground of opulence and indulgence. Most of what can be imagined is or can be right there at a celebrity's fingertips.

The allure of rubbing shoulders with fellow celebrities, influential figures, and industry powerhouses adds an air of exclusivity to everyday experiences. The who, what and where of life becomes as interesting as the how and why. To glimpse a star doing something as "normal" as grocery shopping can be as exciting as seeing them performing their craft. This interest leads to coveted opportunities, such as brand endorsements, lucrative deals, and global recognition, opening doors that most can only dream of. The ability to build an empire out of the aura of being near greatness has proliferated in recent years. Yet the excitement of being in the public eye is not only limited to material perks. It extends to the thrill of living a life less ordinary, where every day brings new adventures and unexpected encounters.

The sense of anticipation that comes with stepping onto a stage or in front of a camera, knowing that all eyes are on you, creates an adrenaline rush that is both exhilarating and nerve-wracking. It is an opportunity to showcase talent, creativity, or unique perspectives, and to leave an indelible mark on the world. Being in the public eye also allows for a platform to make a difference. Celebrities have the power to use their influence for social causes, raising awareness of and rallying support for issues close to their hearts. They can be a voice for those who are marginalized or unheard, leveraging their status to bring about positive change. The ability to impact lives on a large scale is a privilege that comes with the excitement of being in the public eye.

However, along with the excitement and perks, there are also challenges that come with living a public life. The loss of privacy, the constant scrutiny, and the pressure to maintain a flawless image can take a toll on one's mental and emotional well-being. The line between the personal and the public becomes blurred, and navigating the spotlight with grace and authenticity becomes a delicate balancing act. Staying grounded and true to oneself in a world where your every move is on display can be as difficult as finding a genuine support system in a crowd of naysayers or flatterers.

Ultimately, the thrill and perks of being in the public eye are a double-edged sword. They offer incredible opportunities, recognition, and a taste of the extraordinary. Yet this comes with sacrifices, challenges, and a level of scrutiny that few can comprehend.

Stardom is a world of extremes, where the highs are exhilarating, and the lows can be draining. For those who embrace being in the public eye, the excitement and advantages become part of their journey, shaping their lives in profound ways. It is a realm where dreams can be realized, where impact can be made, and where the remarkable becomes the norm. And for those who are drawn to this world, the thrill of being in the public eye will always be an irresistible call, an adventure waiting to unfold. The trials that bring exhaustion or maybe even disruption seem worth undertaking for a chance at greatness.

STRAIGHT from Safaree...

Yo, what's up; it's me, the Stuntman. If anyone knows the real deal about living in the public eye, it's me. This life is like a non-stop rollercoaster, and I'm loving every moment of it. The ups and downs, the thrills, and the excitement—it's a wild ride and you never know what to expect, nor do you want it to end.

There's nothing like the rush of being a celebrity. Everywhere I go, people recognize me and want to meet me and get a glimpse of what I am like. Then there are the flashing cameras—it's like I'm on a never-ending runway show and my every move is digested. That's why I walk with that swagger, you know?

And let's talk about the lifestyle - it's like living a dream. Exotic vacations, VIP parties, and access to the most exclusive events in town are all a part of the package. I get to dine at the fanciest restaurants, party at the hottest clubs, and experience things most people don't even think about.

But it's not just about the stunting. Being in the public eye means I have a voice, and I can use it to make a statement or shed light. Whether it's through my music or my presence on social media, I can reach and connect with my fans. I can inspire and motivate. That's the real power of fame.

There are challenges too: the constant attention, the paparazzi trying to get that perfect shot, and the pressure to always be composed. It's not always easy. But I embrace it all, turning those challenges into opportunities for growth.

Through this wild journey, I stay true to myself, never forgetting where I came from. I have to ignore the critics and haters. I'm here to show the world that no matter what, if you do you, fame can be an incredible ride. So buckle up, because you are about to take a ride like never before, Safaree style!

CHAPTER FOUR

Affairs of the Heart: The Seduction and Temptations of Love On-Set

In the glamorous world of Hollywood, where emotions run high, creativity flows, and dreams come true, the film set becomes a potent breeding ground for feelings—both genuine and deceptive. It's a realm where reality often blurs with fiction, where passionate roles on screen sometimes extend their magnetism off screen. Here, we delve into the tantalizing appeal and treacherous pitfalls of on-set affairs, exploring how the very nature of being on set can create an invigorating yet deceptive alternate reality.

Imagine a sprawling film set, bathed in the soft glow of lights, where talented actors and actresses breathe life into their characters. Stars often prepare for months before shooting to ensure they portray their role just right. Whether that means drastically changing their physical appearance, exposing themselves to a remote location or even mastering a new skill, there are many methods used to get into character. Preparing for a role can also bring new people, whether behind or on screen, into an actor's life, which can transform into a relationship on and off the set. This chemistry, usually between co-stars, often crackles like electricity, their performances drawing audiences into the heart of the story. But what happens when the lines between acting and reality become blurred? The enchanting aura of a film set has a way of erasing boundaries and encouraging a level of intimacy that might not exist in the real world.

On a film set, real life often takes a back seat. The long hours, secluded locations, and intense emotional scenes create an almost dreamlike atmosphere. Other relationships, responsibilities or obligations are often ignored to remain in the zone required to channel the best work. This escapism can make actors more susceptible to developing strong emotional connections with their co-stars. They escape into the roles they play, and sometimes into relationships they never expected.

Actors and actresses, as masters of their craft, become skilled in portraying emotions authentically. When they're called upon to play characters deeply in love, their performances can become so convincing that they believe in the feelings they're portraying. This psychological phenomenon is known as "emotional transference," where the intensity of their performances can spill over into real life. For some, this emotional intensity leads to building intimacy and a sense of vulnerability which ripens the conditions for a connection that transcends the characters. When the feelings can no longer be had, on-set romances can ignite like wildfire.

A set can also offer a haven of secrecy that reinforces the already seductive nature of being on location. Away from the prying eyes of the public or their loved ones, stars can engage in clandestine romances without fear of immediate exposure. Their fellow actors and crew members often respect their privacy, contributing to the allure of forbidden liaisons. This protective world that prioritizes the project enables all those involved to give in to whatever their heart desires and disregard the consequences that may follow.

For some, the chemistry felt on-set cannot be ignored and actually strengthens once back in the real world. The idea that someone understands the lifestyle, the mystique and the pressure that comes with being in the public eye is attractive, even when dealing with daily life. Whether close friendships, fun associations or loving relationships ensue, the set can be a breeding ground for ongoing interconnections between those who co-create a work of art.

However, the dreamlike quality of on-set romances can turn nightmarish when reality comes crashing down. As filming wraps and the real world beckons, the power of the connection can fade. Actors, once deeply entwined in their roles and each other, are forced to grapple with the stark contrast between their on-set lives and their everyday existences. This jarring transition can lead to heartbreak, confusion, and even bitterness. A bond that seemed so strong in the context of the work and shadows fades in the light of day and reality.

Under most circumstances, on-set affairs serve as both a testament to the power of make-believe and a cautionary tale about the complexities of navigating the fine line between fiction and reality. While some on-set romances flourish and lead to lasting relationships, many others remain fleeting encounters—a seductive mirage amidst the dazzling lights of the film industry.

Let's examine a love story that took an unexpected and scandalous turn, captivating the tabloids and gossip columns for months.

Two celebrities, one a charismatic actor known for various roles and the other a rising starlet, were a match made in Hollywood heaven—or so it seemed. Their love story began with the fervor and passion that make headlines. Their red-carpet appearances were a display of unity, smiles, and public affection, leaving fans swooning over the idea of a perfect Hollywood romance.

However, as the saying goes, everything that glitters ain't gold. Behind the scenes, cracks appeared in their perfect relationship. The pressures of fame and a relentless public eye weighed heavily on them. With both celebrities rising in fame, they struggled to find time for each other amidst their hectic schedules. Whispers of arguments and disagreements started making their way into the gossip columns.

Then came the bombshell—the scandal that would rock Hollywood. Reports of infidelity surfaced, alleging that one of them had been involved with a fellow actor while still in a relationship with the other. The tabloids feasted on the story, splashing headlines of betrayal and deceit. Social media erupted, with fans and critics taking sides in the tumultuous saga.

The fallout was swift and brutal. Public opinion turned against the guilty party, and the other found themselves thrust into the spotlight as the wronged partner. The guilty party's career suffered, with many questioning their integrity. The wronged partner received an outpouring of sympathy and support from fans and colleagues.

Despite the storm of controversy, this high-profile couple took a surprising turn. They confronted the scandal head-on. In a candid interview, they spoke openly about their relationship, admitting its flaws and discussing the challenges of fame. They chose therapy and counseling to work through their issues, a move that garnered both praise and skepticism.

Their journey was one of love, betrayal, and ultimately, redemption. While the scandal left an indelible mark on their public personas, it also showcased their resilience and commitment to each other. It's a story that reminds us that love in the public eye is never simple, and that even in the face of scandal, some relationships are worth fighting for.

Peeling back the layers of a high-profile Hollywood scandal offers a glimpse into the complexities of love and fame in the world of celebrities. Their journey, marked by highs and lows, serves as a testament to the enduring power of love, even when it's tested by the harshest of spotlights.

In the world of showbiz, where bright lights and rolling cameras create an intoxicating spectacle, on-set flings have become an open secret, tucked away in the corners of Hollywood's untamed heart. Yet, beyond the drama, a truth prevails: Distance has the power to make hearts wander, even under the scrutiny of the spotlight.

On-set flings are common, as the intensity of movie sets, and TV productions often breed chemistry that transcends the boundaries of the script. The close quarters, the long hours, and the shared passion for storytelling ignite a fire that can be hard to ignore. As cameras roll and directors call out "action," it's not unusual for actors to find themselves swept up in the heat of the moment, their roles on screen blurring with their off-screen desires.

But what begins as an exhilarating on-set connection can quickly lose its luster when the final cut is made. The controlled environment of a set, with its meticulously designed scenes and tightly managed schedules, creates a semblance of an alternate reality that is deceiving. It's an illusion that leaves actors and crew members wondering if the sparks they felt on-set can translate to a lasting connection in the real world.

In the world of entertainment, distance is an omnipresent force. Actors may find themselves whisked away to new projects in far-flung locations, separated by oceans and continents. The hectic schedules, the constant travel, and the glare of public attention can create an emotional chasm that is challenging to bridge. The initial attraction that flared on set may flicker and wane when confronted with the stark reality of a long-distance relationship.

As time passes and distance grows, the allure of novelty can prove irresistible. New projects bring new faces, and the thrill of a fresh on-set connection beckons like a siren's call. Hearts once entangled in the heat of passion on one set may drift and seek new flames to kindle.

In Hollywood and beyond, affairs born on set and relationships tested by distance are not unique, but a reflection of the complex, emotional landscape traversed by those in the entertainment industry. As cameras stop rolling and reality sets in, individuals must grapple with the human challenges of longing, temptation, and pursuing a genuine connection. In a world where glamour and reality coexist, the hearts of those who walk the red carpet remain as vulnerable and as hopeful as any other.

STRAIGHT from Safaree...

Affairs of the heart are something I know all too well. And nothing is sexier than the temptation of a new and unpredictable on-set romance. Trust me, it's a wild ride.

When you're on set, whether it's television or a music video, you're surrounded by talented and attractive people. It's like a playground for grownups, and sometimes those lines between work and play can get blurry. I've seen it happen to the best of us, even me. You're working closely with someone, the chemistry is off the charts, and before you know it, sparks are flying. It's exhilarating, but it can also be dangerous.

The entertainment industry thrives on drama, and a little scandal can go a long way in the headlines. But as someone who's been through it all, let me caution that the price of these affairs can be steep. It's not just about the potential damage to your career or reputation – it's the emotional toll it takes. Affairs of the heart can lead to heartbreak, trust issues, and a whole lot of drama you didn't sign up for.

But here's the thing: I've also seen beautiful love stories emerge from the chaos of on-set temptations. Sometimes you find that real, deep connection with someone you're working with, and it's worth exploring. So whether you're in the spotlight or navigating your own affairs of the heart, remember to stay true to yourself and your values. It's a seductive world out there, but ultimately, it's the choices you make that define your journey. Stay tuned for more on that from yours truly.

CHAPTER FIVE

Tabloid Entanglements: Media's Impact on Celebrity Relationships

The realm where celebrities' love stories unfold under the watchful gaze of the public and the relationship between fame and affection form a complex and captivating tale. Like modern-day gold prospectors, paparazzi are known for chasing moments that promise not just a glimpse into the lives of the famous, but also the allure of unimaginable wealth.

Historically, these photographers have struck gold with a single candid shot, a photograph that could rewrite the course of history. Icons like famous actresses and actors have become immortalized in flashbulbs, their lives rewritten by the shutter clicks of those seeking to make millions. The art of capturing these moments wasn't merely a trade; it was a claim to fame.

But within the dazzling realm of stardom, love stories emerge that rival the splendor of Hollywood itself. Couples, often titans, find themselves ensnared in a relentless spotlight. While the world adores their unions, the media's glare casts an eternal shadow, forcing them to navigate the treacherous waters of fame while preserving the sanctity of their love.

Beneath the façade of flashing lights, however, darker forces are at play. Rumors and baseless allegations emerge like typhoons, threatening to dismantle even the most robust relationships. The stress and strain of constant scrutiny become unwelcome companions, testing the resilience of couples who must strive to keep their love afloat amidst a sea of doubt.

In today's digital age, the paparazzi's influence extends far beyond their cameras. Social media becomes an amplifier, projecting their narratives to a global audience. A single image or tweet can ignite wildfires of speculation, subjecting celebrities to the overwhelming power of the online world.

For some celebrities, the breaking point arrives, and they take a stand. Invasion of their privacy, the most sacred boundary, becomes a line that cannot be crossed with impunity. The courtroom becomes the battleground where celebrities and paparazzi engage in a fierce legal dance, seeking justice and safeguarding their personal lives.

Yet, amid the chaos and controversy, the allure of celebrity dating remains an undeniable force. The world watches in fascination as power couples emerge and love stories unfold beneath the relentless spotlight. Despite the trials and tribulations, some relationships not only endure but also flourish, showing resilience and reminding us that love, even under the brightest of spotlights, remains an indomitable force.

In this fascinating realm of fame and love, the impact of paparazzi, media scrutiny, rumors, and scandals on relationships unfolds in a captivating saga. It's a testament to the resilience of the human heart, the magnetic appeal of romance in the public eye, and pursuing love, even amidst the flashing cameras and sensational headlines.

Celebrities, juggling hectic schedules and glamorous encounters, often find their love lives intertwined with tabloid gossip. These publications construct narratives from minuscule fragments of information, sometimes exposing errors or genuine scandals before couples can address them privately. Regaining control of their own narrative becomes a challenge, leaving their relationships exposed.

Navigating love in this environment has a way of magnifying insecurities and sparking unexpected drama. Even the strongest couples face scrutiny over their appearances, public chemistry, and life choices. The media spares no aspect of their lives.

In this realm, rumors and scandals are potential minefields, threatening even the most resilient relationships as couples confront external judgments and their own vulnerabilities. These stories serve as a poignant reminder that love, even in the world of fame and fortune, faces the same trials as any other.

One thing is abundantly clear: Love in the public eye is a mesmerizing yet demanding journey. It showcases the strength of the human spirit under the relentless glare of the media's spotlight. The unrelenting paparazzi and the ever-churning rumor mill can affect even the most passionate celebrity relationships.

It serves as a stark reminder that love, under the unyielding gaze of the spotlight, can be both a blessing and a curse. Even the most unbreakable bonds can tremble beneath the weight of public perception.

Let's shift our focus to how Safaree encountered the unrelenting gaze of the paparazzi and media scrutiny, and how these trials pushed the boundaries of love and trust to celebrity limits.

STRAIGHT from Safaree...

In this wild world of music and reality TV, I found myself right in the center of fame, fortune, and the relentless media spotlight. My journey, especially during my time on *Love & Hip Hop*, laid bare the profound effects of paparazzi attention and media scrutiny on personal relationships. As we dive into my experiences and this narrative, just know that we're about to unravel the intricate dance between a celebrity's life and the enduring essence of love, resilience, and the unbreakable human spirit.

As I climbed the ladder of fame, my life morphed into an open book, accessible to anyone with a camera or a keyboard. Every move I made, from public outings to those intimate moments, was under constant surveillance. Paparazzi, those ever-present hounds of the celebrity world, became an inescapable part of my daily existence. They trailed my steps, capturing candid shots and moments I wished could remain private.

With the fame of reality TV came a unique notoriety – the type that exposed not only my career but also my personal life. My romantic relationships became fodder for tabloids and gossip columns. The paparazzi seemed to have an uncanny ability to be in the right place at the right time, turning my moments of vulnerability into front-page headlines.

One incident that still resonates involved a whirlwind of rumors and speculations about my romantic involvement with another high-profile figure. The media pounced on these rumors with gusto, crafting sensational stories that played out in the public eye. Social media, with its uncensored opinions and judgments, only amplified the buzz.

In this media frenzy, my partner and I navigated treacherous waters. Our trust, the cornerstone of any relationship, suddenly felt fragile, tested by external pressures and an unrelenting news cycle. We grappled with misunderstandings fueled by the distorted lens of public scrutiny. The burden of having to defend and safeguard our relationship bore down on us.

Amidst the cacophony of competing voices vying for recognition, my unwavering love for music and steadfast commitment to my career acted as an anchor during the relentless storm.

CHAPTER SIX

Power Couples PR

Public relations professionals are often the unsung heroes in the world of celebrity relationships. They work tirelessly behind the scenes, managing crises, shaping narratives, and making sure the celebrity couple's image remains pristine. When rumors circulate or scandals threaten to erupt, it's the PR team that steps in to mitigate damage and protect the carefully crafted image of the power couple.

While celebrity PR companies are adept at damage control, some situations defy containment, taking on a life of their own. This example illustrates a scenario that spiraled beyond anyone's control, defying even the best PR efforts.

Not too long ago, there was a high-profile couple, both A-list celebrities who seemed to have it all: fame, fortune, and a picture-perfect relationship. Let's call them Couple X. They had a devoted fan base, lucrative endorsement deals, and a carefully cultivated image of being the "perfect" couple.

However, behind the scenes, their relationship was far from perfect. Rumors of infidelity and discord had swirled for some time, but the PR team had kept a tight lid on these whispers. They had successfully downplayed any signs of trouble and projected an image of unity and bliss.

Then, one fateful evening, it all unraveled. An anonymous source leaked incriminating text messages between one half of Couple X and a third party. The messages left no room for interpretation - infidelity was undeniable.

Within hours, the scandal had gone viral. The public was relentless in its pursuit of the truth, and the media frenzy was unlike anything Couple X had ever experienced. The carefully crafted image they had maintained for years began to crumble.

The PR team was in overdrive, trying to manage the crisis. They issued statements denying the allegations, and they even considered legal action against the source of the leak. But the damage was done, and the public was unforgiving. Social media was ablaze with commentary, and fans felt betrayed.

As the scandal continued to dominate headlines, endorsement deals started to vanish. Sponsors distanced themselves from Couple X, and fans canceled their support. The pressure intensified, leading to a breaking point in their relationship.

Despite their best efforts to weather the storm, Couple X eventually made the painful decision to part ways. The breakup became a public spectacle, with every detail analyzed and dissected by the media. Their once-gleaming image was tarnished beyond repair.

This story serves as a stark reminder that, in the world of celebrity relationships, there are moments when even the most skilled PR teams can't salvage a situation. When a scandal reaches a certain magnitude, it becomes a force of its own, and the fallout can be devastating.

To sum it up, celebrity relationships are a fascinating mix of real emotions, careful planning, and the tricky world of public image. It's a place where true feelings meet the need to look good to the public, and where everything they do is watched by millions. Couple X's story is a great example of both the dangers and the enduring fascination of this world, where love and fame come together in ways that always grab our attention.

In this special world, love isn't just a private feeling – it's a public strategy. Celebrities' lives, from who they date to what they post on social media, become part of a bigger story that shapes their careers and how people see them. It's a world where they must balance being real with looking good and keeping that balance under constant public scrutiny is an art form.

Behind the scenes, PR experts work tirelessly to manage how celebrities are seen. They protect their reputations, handle crises, and try to keep the public image of power couples safe. But as we saw in Couple X's story, even the best PR can't always fix things when a big scandal happens.

The world of celebrity relationships is a place where we see the mix of real feelings and the need to look good in public. It's a fascinating world where the most personal parts of life are always connected to the public's expectations. Couple X's story reminds us that this world has its risks but will always keep us intrigued with its unique blend of love and fame.

STRAIGHT from Safaree...

Navigating the intricate world of celebrity relationships is no easy feat. While love may be the driving force behind any union, there's often much more at play when two high-profile figures come together. Enter the realm of Power Couples and PR, a realm where strategic celebrity pairings are carefully curated for image and influence, and where the role of public relations takes center stage.

For someone like me, who's no stranger to the glitzy world of fame, the dynamics of dating in the public eye bring their own set of challenges and opportunities. It's a dance where love meets strategy, and public relations plays a pivotal role in shaping the narrative.

When two influential individuals in the entertainment industry unite, it's not just a personal journey—it's a carefully calculated move that can enhance their status, elevate their careers, and even align them with particular brands or causes. The choices we make as a couple become strategic decisions, and every public appearance, social media post, or interview is orchestrated to convey a specific image.

Having firsthand experience with high-profile relationships, I understand the importance of perception in the public eye. Whether it's stepping out together at high-profile events, collaborating on projects, or even using our relationship as a platform to champion social causes, celebrity couples like me bring intentionality to every aspect of our partnership.

But while the world may see the polished exterior of these power couples, the reality behind the scenes can be vastly different. I know that the scrutiny of the public eye can take a toll on personal relationships. Maintaining a healthy balance between public image and private life is an ongoing challenge—one that requires a delicate blend of authenticity and strategic messaging.

CHAPTER SEVEN

Reality TV Romances

In today's world, where the line between real life and entertainment blurs more with each passing day, reality television has captured not just our attention but our hearts. It's a place where the authenticity of relationships is put under the spotlight, and where love, in all its complexities, plays out in front of millions. So let's explore the captivating world of reality television romances, where emotions are real, but the cameras are always rolling.

There's an undeniable allure to watching love unfold on the small screen. The rawness, vulnerability, and sheer unpredictability of it all are downright addictive. Reality TV, with its diverse range of shows, from dating competitions to relationship-focused docuseries, gives us a front-row seat to the entire spectrum of human emotions. Scripted characters have their place, but reality duos win the prize regarding fanaticism. The draw to reality television characters is undeniable and we root for them above all odds.

Franchises like *Love & Hip Hop* have become household staples, offering a glimpse into the turbulent love lives of hip-hop's finest.

The drama, the passion, and the real-life conflicts are magnetic, taking viewers away from their own mundane and ordinary lives. These shows are a glimpse into the everyday life of those who are presented as larger-than-life characters. But the true attraction to reality television is that we now know these people—how they think, love and act. The empathy built out of this connection is strong and is even stronger when reality stars fall in love with each other. It is common for genuine relationships to blossom on reality television, and that's a testament to their compelling storytelling. Viewers begin to identify with their struggles, obstacles and triumphs. The important milestones in the lives of reality stars are celebrated along with them, enmeshing the relationship even further. The secret thought that truly excites many watchers is that maybe the next up-and-coming star could be them, a love story waiting at the other end.

Speaking of captivating shows, *The Real Housewives* series has taken us into the sensational lives of affluent women. It's a whirlwind of luxury, drama, and opulence, while also bringing an aspect of misbehaving and violating social norms. These areas seem to contradict high end meets aggressive, but it is fascinating to watch those whom we expect to behave good act bad. And beneath it all, these shows have showcased real and relatable moments of connection and love. They remind us that even amidst extravagant parties and high-society events, genuine bonds can form, making us feel more connected to their world.

For all its entertainment value and real-world success stories, reality TV love isn't without its skeptics. Many viewers question the authenticity of these relationships, wondering if they're merely ploys for ratings and fame. It's a valid concern, as the pressure of the cameras and the promise of public recognition can undoubtedly influence behavior. However, reality TV is a unique beast. It places ordinary people in extraordinary situations, often designed to provoke emotional responses. Stars are under constant scrutiny, and their reactions to various challenges are captured for the world to see. The very nature of reality TV can lead to moments that feel manufactured, even when the emotions are real.

Yet we've already seen how on-set life can set the stage for affairs, trysts, and true love, so it is not surprising that the filming of reality series brings about these different connections. The only difference is these stars allow the cameras and media to be along for the ride, notwithstanding the consequences that may also be a part of the documentation.

What keeps us coming back, season after season, is the unpredictability of love. Despite the odds, despite the skeptical viewers, genuine connections form. The magic of reality TV romance lies in the fact that, amidst all the orchestrated moments and artificial drama, love, in its most authentic form, can blossom. And in the off chance it occurs, viewers are captivated.

Reality television provides a modern lens through which we can examine love and relationships. It reminds us that love can be messy, complicated, and even unpredictable. Whether it's watching a couple's journey on *Love & Hip Hop* or witnessing the trials and tribulations of relationships on *The Real Housewives*, these shows offer a reflection of our own experiences with love, but in a more dramatic and often sensationalized manner.

Reality TV romances, with all their flaws and manufactured moments, still captivate us because they tap into our universal fascination with human connection and love. They remind us that, even amidst drama and catfighting, struggles and scrutiny, genuine connections can form, and real emotions can surface. These shows have a unique way of making us feel connected to the lives and loves of those on screen. So as the cameras keep rolling and the drama unfolds, we'll keep tuning in because it's all about the unpredictable, unscripted nature of love.

STRAIGHT from Safaree...

You know, there's somethin' special 'bout reality TV romances that just hooks people in, and I totally get it, man. These shows bring together regular folks, everyday individuals, and toss 'em into the whirlwind world of love, right there on your screen.

One reason it's got that undeniable appeal is because it's relatable. You feel me? These ain't folks with their lives under the microscope; these are ordinary individuals navigating the messy terrain of dating. It's like watchin' your own romantic adventures unfold, with all the thrilling highs and heart-wrenching lows.

But here's the real kicker - the drama. Reality TV knows how to serve it up. They throw in unexpected twists, turns, and surprises that keep you on the edge of your seat. It's an emotional rollercoaster, and you wonder what's comin' next.

Yet it's not only 'bout the love story. It's also 'bout the people themselves. You get to know these individuals—their quirks, their imperfections—and you become invested in their personal growth journey. You start rootin' for your favorite, celebrate their wins, and empathize with their struggles.

And life can sometimes throw you curveballs too. When you tune in to reality TV romances, it's like takin' a breather from the real world and divin' into a realm filled with glitz, glamour, and yes, a touch of chaos. It's like a brief mental getaway, a chance to escape the ordinary and immerse yourself in a universe where love takes the spotlight.

So this fascination with reality TV romances is genuine, and it's here to stay. It's a celebration of human connection, a front-row seat to captivatin' drama, and a temporary escape from the everyday grind. In a world that's sometimes too predictable, these shows remind us that love, with all its ups and downs, remains one of life's most unpredictable adventures, ya dig?

CHAPTER EIGHT

Navigating Love in the Digital Age

Romance and relationships can be electrifying in this digital age. The rise of technology, especially social media, has transformed everything we thought we knew about love. Love in the digital age has evolved with even more complexity, bursting with new possibilities and challenges. Information, access and connection can now occur in the blink of an eye without the limitations of geography or circumstance. However, distractions, comparisons and boundless options set the stage for a frenzy.

Now imagine you're a celebrity, someone whose life is under a constant magnifying glass. Your love life is no longer your own; it's a global spectacle. You've become a master at navigating the delicate dance between public exposure and the sanctuary of your relationship. It's a tightrope walk, and you're right in the spotlight. And you not only have to be careful about what you do, you must also manage the behavior of those close to you. One post, one picture or one wrong move, and your life is forever changed.

But here's the twist: The pressure is also on to craft the perfect image of yourself as well as your relationship. You're adored by millions, and every move you make is scrutinized. So you take to social media, turning it into your canvas. You paint a picture of grand gestures, luxurious getaways, and glamorous events. Yet amidst all this glitter, you face the challenge of keeping your love story authentic and vulnerable.

Then the digital tempest arrives. Rumors and scandals whirl around you at dizzying speeds. Accusations of infidelity, doubts about the genuineness of your love—nothing is off-limits. Whether the reports are real, misinformed or straight-up lies, the information has the chance to affect your character and your image. Your responses to these storms not only affect your love life but also have far-reaching consequences for your career and public image.

But it's not all turbulence; there's a silver lining. Social media acts as a bridge, connecting you with your partner and your global fanbase. The ability to make an impact and expand your reach can evolve overnight. It's a platform where you share moments of profound affection, champion shared causes, and fortify your bond in the digital realm. Your digital presence not only becomes a testament to who you are, but the way you see and express love online creates a digital sense of togetherness.

It's not all sunshine; trolls lurk in the digital shadows. Negative comments and hurtful judgments abound, often extending to your relationship. Handling this digital negativity becomes an art form. You learn to master the art of ignoring the noise, using strategic measures like blocking, or carefully curating your social media spaces. However, that does not come naturally to most, especially stars whose entire creative existence is built on the opinions of others. Mastering the skill of disregarding the thoughts of the masses, even the fans, is difficult if not impossible for most celebrities.

Yet to maintain a successful love life in the spotlight, there is no way around growing thick skin and understanding you can't win them all. The success of dating and relating in the digital age rests in the balance of transparency and privacy: what you show the world versus what your relationship is.

Now shift your gaze to everyday individuals. They traverse this digital landscape too, with their own unique experiences and challenges. They use social media to connect with potential partners, navigating dating apps and virtual meet-cutes. But they also face the daunting task of measuring their own relationships against the seemingly perfect love stories they encounter online, leading to insecurities and self-doubt.

And in a world of filters and photo editing, distinguishing authenticity from illusion becomes a puzzle for everyone. Couples, like you, are pressured to present a narrative of perfection on social media while staying true to their genuine experiences, including the inevitable ups and downs.

Another part of the digital landscape is the constant barrage of data, news and media. The fear of missing out has taken over and smartphones are almost glued to our hands. The distractions of the world and others' lives begin to prevent us from living our own lives, whether in or out of the spotlight. The person right in front of you is no longer the focus and looking outward becomes a habit. It is nearly impossible to form a true connection or build trust and intimacy without the proper attention and focus. But it is hard to be vulnerable with someone whose eyes are on the screen; quality time off the screen is needed.

The influence of social media on love, the impact on both celebrities and everyday people, is far reaching. It's a narrative of how we connect, communicate, and cultivate relationships in this digital age. Whether in the dazzling spotlight of fame or the quiet corners of everyday life, love remains a shared human experience. It's about genuine emotions and connections that bind us. Amidst the digital fireworks, love, with all its imperfections, continues to shine as a guiding light in the ever-evolving landscape of modern romance.

STRAIGHT from Safaree...

Hey, it's your boy Safaree, and I've got to share something that's turned love upside down - dating in the digital era. It's like a whole new universe out here, and if you're not doing it right, you might find yourself lost in the shuffle. So let me lay it out for you, Safaree-style.

In this digital era, your first impression doesn't happen in person; it's right there on your phone screen. Your profile picture, that clever bio - they're your tickets to this dating game. Get them right, or you'll find yourself ignored, deleted or swiped left before you even say "hello."

Now let's talk about the Swipe Life. Dating apps? You know 'em. Swipe right if you're vibing with someone, swipe left if it's a no-go. It's like a virtual club, and you're choosing your dance partner. When you match, it's like the universe giving you a nudge, saying, "Hey, check this out." One minute you can be working or traveling and the next be caught up in a new virtual link. But it can fizzle as fast as it excites from one strange response or one false move. There is nothing like the excitement and the possibilities of a new connection.

Texting becomes your superpower in the digital dating world. Emojis, GIFs, and those moments that literally make you LOL - they're all a part of the charm. You've got to know how to keep that conversation flowing like a smooth melody.

But here's the real challenge: finding the balance. You can't live on your phone forever. You match with someone, and now what?

Balancing the digital world and real-life interactions is where the adventure begins. Too much screen time, and you'll be stuck in a never-ending text saga. Move too fast, and you might crash and burn.

Now, let's get into some dating lingo: **Ghosting** is when someone you've been chatting with suddenly vanishes into thin air – no replies, no goodbyes, just radio silence. **Benching** is like you're on the sidelines, waiting for your turn while they explore other options. Hopefully, you're the one doing the ghosting and benching; if not, get correct. But don't worry—the dating world can be wild and unpredictable, so things could change in a moment.

But here's a crucial note: safety first. When you meet someone from the digital world, stick to public places. Your personal info isn't something to toss around like confetti. You aren't trying to have just everybody knowing your information, your favorite spots or where they can find you later. If something feels off, trust your gut; it's your best compass. Everybody doesn't have the best intentions.

Now, the paradox of choice: Sometimes, having too many options can be too much. You're running through DMs or swiping through profiles like you're browsing a restaurant menu. But remember, it's not about quantity, unless it is! If you're really trying to find someone cool to chill with, it's about finding that quality connection.

And I can't stress this enough: Authenticity is key. The digital world might tempt you to become someone you're not, to represent yourself how you think you should appear. But staying true to yourself is where the real magic happens. Catfishing isn't cool, and pretending to be someone else won't lead you to genuine love.

What about long-distance? It's possible now. Video calls, texting, quick flights – they bring you together, even if you're miles apart. Even if you're crossing borders, it's all good. Digital connections transcend boundaries, introducing you to people from diverse backgrounds and cultures. It's a chance to learn, explore, and find love in unexpected places.

In the grand scheme of dating in the digital era, it's like a new Chapter in the book of love. There's a unique rhythm to it, a vibe all its own. Embrace it, stay true to yourself, and remember that it's all about discovering that authentic connection in a world that's tech obsessed. Keep DMing, keep swiping, keep texting, but above all, keep believing in love. It's out there, waiting for you to find it.

CHAPTER NINE

Secret Trysts: Private Affairs versus Public Image

Today, in the world of fame and fortune, power is the name of the game. The influence it carries opens doors to luxurious experiences, high-profile events, and the capacity to shape others' careers. But when you're in a relationship with another high-profile figure there's always that nagging doubt—are they using their reach to manipulate situations, hide affairs, or entangle themselves in secretive encounters? Are they convincing others to keep silent on things that would expose what they do behind closed doors to seem upstanding or in control of their own narrative?

Let's be real here: Who among us hasn't ventured into the realm of a thrilling fantasy involving a beloved celebrity? We begin crafting these daydreams, picturing whirlwind romances, but there's a catch—they must remain clandestine, concealed from the public eye. Envision it: passionate encounters with a star, journeys to exotic locales, all veiled in secrecy. It's the kind of narrative that seldom materializes, yet the mere contemplation of it quickens the pulse. Now what if I revealed that the sole barrier between you and transforming these reveries into reality is a commitment to maintain absolute discretion, far from the prying gazes and the rumor mills?

It's a tempting proposition, no doubt. This is the very foundation of many secret trysts—the allure of power, the thrill of the forbidden, and the satisfaction of having something for you. Or maybe you even let your thoughts run wild imagining what the future may hold or what else may come to pass, but you force yourself to enjoy the moment. In the realm where fame and desire collide, secret rendezvous and concealed affairs are the threads that weave an intricate tapestry. These experiences add a layer of complexity to the lives of celebrities in love, a world I've navigated.

The affairs come in many forms, from clandestine exchanges on social media to passionate encounters with devoted fans during tours. Sometimes they involve the excitement of new love interests or even the electrifying chemistry between reality stars caught in the glitzy whirlwind of stardom—a look between takes, a touch at an event or more. In this world, secrets are currency, and discretion is paramount. This is another side of the thrilling yet perilous dance of desire and discretion that defines the lives of celebrities.

Regarding fame and secrecy, stories are whispered in hidden corners, tales rarely admitted, yet undeniably enticing. It's about a celebrity who is enchanted by the forbidden fruit they encounter at a lavish celebrity bash or while on tour. What starts as a tasteful essence of temptation can quickly spiral into a seductive and lust-filled encounter.

Imagine a superstar, accustomed to the glitz and glamour of the celebrity scene, where temptation often lurks behind the scenes, attending extravagant parties, meeting captivating people, and tasting the forbidden fruits. What seems like an innocent flirtation can ignite an uncontrollable passion. Secret encounters are like a flame in the dark, irresistible and dangerous. Each stolen moment is an intoxicating descent into desire, a whirlwind of emotions that defies logic. The chemistry between you is magnetic, pulling you closer with a force you can't resist.

But the cloak of secrecy is a heavy burden. You live in constant fear of being caught, of ruining a happy home, a reputation or even a business deal. You begin weaving a web of lies to cover your tracks or creating the perfect opportunities to do what you want to do and be where you really want to be. It's a dangerous game of suspense. The thrill of the hidden meetings is tainted by the guilt that shadows them, but not enough to stop. Not now.

But when one celebrity eventually wants to end it, things can get tricky. The affair, once passionate and seductive, can turn messy and perhaps dangerous. We've seen this with many celebrities, athletes, and public figures. An affair that began secretly now threatens to become a scandal that grabs headlines.

The jilted lover may not want to let go, resorting to unpredictable actions—damaged cars, broken windows, constant calls, online stalking, and even attempts to contact the celebrity's significant other if one exists—as desperate attempts to hold on.

In the most extreme cases, extortion becomes a weapon in this high-stakes battle of secrets. Threats to expose the affair, reveal intimate details to the media, or air the celebrity's dirty laundry on social media turn the situation into an undesirable standoff. Some go to great lengths to avoid exposure of their actions, while others choose a well-managed reveal of the truth before the web of lies can bring them down any further.

Despite a past filled with learning lessons of prior celebrity scandals and falls from grace or even tragic headlines showcased, the infatuation with sexy trysts or long-standing affairs continues. It is a complex journey filled with seduction and risk. Trying to end such affairs can lead to explosive and sometimes harmful consequences. Yet secrets hold significant sway, often demanding a price far beyond anyone's expectations.

Now let's explore an example that vividly illustrates the enticing appeal and risky nature of these hidden affairs.

In a recent scandal that sent shockwaves through the entertainment world, a well-known athlete found himself embroiled in controversy with an exotic dancer to whom he had become addicted. The story began innocently enough, as they crossed paths at an upscale nightclub, their worlds colliding in a haze of dimmed lights and pulsating music.

What started as a chance encounter soon evolved into a clandestine affair, hidden from prying eyes. The exotic dancer, drawn to the allure of the athlete's fame and fortune, saw an opportunity for a taste of the high life. Their secret rendezvous became a thrilling and perilous dance of desire; each time they met flames of passion increased.

However, as time passed, the dancer's desires grew increasingly extravagant. She yearned for more than stolen moments in the shadows; she wanted a slice of the celebrity's wealth and status. When her demands were not met, the situation spiraled out of control.

Frustration gave way to vindictiveness, and what was once a secret affair threatened to explode into a public scandal. Threats of exposure, damaging revelations, and attempts to leverage the situation for financial gain cast a dark shadow over the affair.

The athlete, addicted to her sauce and trapped in a web of deceit and manipulation, navigated treacherous waters. His career, reputation, and personal life hung in the balance as he grappled with the fallout of this affair gone awry.

This scandal serves as a stark reminder of the dangers lurking in the world of secret trysts, where desire can quickly turn into a volatile and destructive force. It's a cautionary tale of how clandestine affairs, when driven by addiction, greed, and manipulation, can threaten to consume the lives of those involved.

STRAIGHT from Safaree…

Yo, let me lay it out straight for you, especially regarding these hidden affairs and keeping things on the down-low in the entertainment world. I've seen my fair share, and it's like walking a tightrope while juggling flaming swords, believe me.

In the limelight, temptation is everywhere. You could be at a party, a show, or even just chillin', and bam, sparks start flyin'. Now, I ain't judgin' anyone – we're all human; we all feel that pull sometimes.

But here's the deal, once you step into that secret affair territory, it's a whole new game. Privacy becomes your best friend because your public image, the one you've been building up, is on the line.

It's not just about the thrill of those secret meetups; it's about the risk. You're playin' with fire, ridin' the line between desire and disaster. And disaster can come knockin' real quick.

I've seen it firsthand, man. When these affairs come to light, it's like a bomb went off. It ain't about the people involved; it's front-page news, and your career? Well, it's sittin' on a shaky foundation.

Now, I'm not here to preach. We all make choices, and sometimes they lead us down tricky paths. But in this industry, where every move is under a microscope, those choices can change your life in an instant.

So when you're in this game, you're constantly walkin' that tightrope. You gotta know when to step back, when to resist temptation, and understand that every move you make can shake the ground beneath you.

It's a high-stakes game, my friends, and finding that balance between keepin' your private life private and maintainin' that polished public image ain't no joke. But it's a lesson learned in the school of hard knocks, and it's a reality we face in this entertainment world.

CHAPTER TEN

Fractured Fairy Tales: Celebrity Breakups in the Spotlight

In the luminous world of entertainment, where the glitz and glamour often obscure the harsh realities of life, one aspect of celebrity existence captivates our collective attention like a wildfire – the exhilarating highs and devastating lows of heartbreak in love. The zenith of a celebrity relationship can feel like they're brushing the heavens, but inevitably, what soars can descend. And let's be brutally honest: Few things incite our curiosity more than the dissolution of a once-envied celebrity power couple.

When the star-studded bonds we idolized shatter, the world craves every morsel of information, every intimate detail about what went awry, who started the breakup, and the emotional wreckage left in its wake. It's as if, for a moment, we forget these celebrities, who typically live their lives in the glaring spotlight, are real human beings, subject to the same emotional turmoil as the rest of us. The situation is intellectualized and the hurt that likely exists is ignored for being a part of the conversation and ingesting whatever details spill.

But what does heartbreak look like in the unforgiving arena of fame? Picture this: the all-consuming pain etched on a celebrity's face splattered across every television screen and smart device as they grapple with the end of a love story that the world once celebrated. Imagine their sleepless nights, haunted by the relentless echoes of a love lost, while the media and paparazzi tail them at every corner, snapping photos and probing for scraps of emotion to serve as headline fodder. Or even worse, holding up in place yet seeing the face of their ex anytime they look around.

On social media, where nothing is sacred, heartbreak isn't a private matter; it becomes a public spectacle. As the paparazzi shadow their every move, capturing raw moments of despair and plastering them across glossy tabloid covers, the anguish intensifies. Imagine having your heartache turned into a commodity, a form of entertainment for the masses, where your most vulnerable moments are reduced to paparazzi snapshots and sensational headlines.

Every anguished post, every cryptic message, and every tearful interview becomes a part of the narrative. Celebrities are subjected to an unrelenting barrage of comments, both supportive and callous, from strangers dissecting their pain in real-time. It's a level of scrutiny and vulnerability that most of us can't fathom, and yet celebrities endure it. This is one of the many prices paid to remain a star, and the world comes to collect.

The aftermath of heartbreak in the public eye is a tumultuous journey. Celebrities must navigate a minefield of emotions while being scrutinized, judged, and often ridiculed by the world. Even if there are supporters, the constant barrage of questions and speculation when trying to move forward, or forget for one moment, is like a weight holding them back. Coping with such a deeply personal loss while the relentless spotlight shines on you is a Herculean task, one that often requires stepping away from the glare of fame, even if only temporarily, to heal wounds that the public eye can't see.

When love and heartbreak are dissected like pieces of art on display, celebrities face the monumental challenge of preserving their emotional wellbeing. For them, heartbreak isn't a private affair; it's a spectacle that unfolds in front of a global audience, a relentless, unforgiving force that demands resilience, strength, and, above all, the courage to heal amidst the blinding lights of fame.

STRAIGHT from Safaree...

Picture this: You're a public figure, and your every move is dissected by fans, critics, and the ever-present paparazzi. When your relationship is soaring, the world celebrates your love story, showering you with admiration and envy. Even the haters are easy to ignore as you are on Cloud 9, enjoying the happy moments in public and private. But when that love story begins to unravel, the minute people catch wind that the relationship may be in decline, it's as if the world holds its breath, waiting for the dramatic fallout.

For me, it's been a rollercoaster ride through the highs and lows of romance. When I've found love, the world watched with fascination. When that love crumbled, the world held its breath, eager to know the intricate details of what went wrong. And the aftermath of a Hollywood heartbreak is unlike anything you can imagine.

When you're in the spotlight, heartache isn't private; it's a spectacle that plays out on the grand stage of tabloids, social media, and endless headlines. Imagine having your most intimate moments, the raw emotions of a breakup, laid bare for the world to see. Your pain becomes entertainment, your tears become clickbait, and your vulnerability is exposed to an unforgiving audience.

In the era of social media, break-ups now take on a new dimension. Every post, every comment, and every cryptic message becomes a piece of the puzzle that fans and followers eagerly try to decipher. It's as if the world becomes a collective therapist, analyzing your every move and offering unsolicited advice. Coping with heartache is challenging enough but doing it under this intense scrutiny in the eyes of the world is an unforgiving beast.

As paparazzi cameras flash relentlessly, capturing your most vulnerable moments, the anguish deepens. Imagine trying to heal while the world watches your pain unfold in real time. Your grief becomes a commodity, your emotional turmoil a source of entertainment, and your quest for closure is a public spectacle.

But here's the thing about heartache in the spotlight—it forces you to find strength you never knew you had. It compels you to rebuild, to reinvent yourself, and to emerge from the ashes of a failed love story stronger and wiser. It's a journey of self-discovery, resilience, and ultimately healing.

Even in the brightest lights, there are shadows of pain and loss. But in those shadows, we find the courage to heal, the strength to move forward, and the determination to reclaim our happiness, no matter how public the heartache may be.

CHAPTER ELEVEN

Spinning the Block: Rekindled Romances and Second Chances

When celebrity love affairs are splashed across tabloids and social media, nothing captures our collective attention more than a couple giving love another shot. It's like watching a high-stakes drama unfold before our eyes, with naysayers and hopeful romantics battling it out in the court of public opinion.

Picture this: A high-profile couple has called it quits, their breakup making headlines and fueling endless speculation. The messy details of their separation become headlines for gossip magazines, and it seems like they've moved on to become each other's number one enemy. And even if it is not a contemptuous breakup, it eventually seems they have stopped caring altogether. We await any sign or signal that things are not over, for good or for bad, as that is the worst ending. But then, just when we thought their love story had reached its final chapter, they rekindle the flame.

The world watches with bated breath as they take that daring step toward reconciliation. It may start with a comment on a post, a night out amongst a group or attending the same event. The public is quick to catch wind that a favorite celebrity pair has fallen back to old patterns, or they are orbiting the same locations. And fans watch closely for more details or proof that things may be back on.

Will they be able to forgive each other for past mistakes? Can they rebuild the trust shattered during their breakup? Have they grown and learned from their past, or are they headed for heartbreak once again?

These are the questions that swirl around rekindled celebrity romances. It's a risky move. When you've experienced the rollercoaster of a high-profile breakup, you're not just dealing with your own emotions; you're navigating the opinions and judgments of an entire audience. So many emotions, so many invested, so much on the line—where will things go from here?

But there's something undeniably captivating about second chances in love. It's a testament to the enduring power of human connection, the idea that love can be rekindled even in the most challenging of circumstances. Seeing celebrities who once seemed destined for heartbreak now taking a chance on each other gives hope. Hope that one day they will find love. Hope that their current relationship withstands ups and downs. Hope that love does conquer all.

For these couples, the journey back to love is often a rocky one. They face not only the usual challenges of any relationship but also the weight of their past mistakes and the ever-watchful eye of the public. But in this vulnerability, they find their strength, their determination to make it work this time, and their commitment to building a future together.

Rekindling a romance is a testament to the human capacity for change, growth, and the enduring allure of second chances. It's a journey that teaches us that, with dedication and self-reflection, love can conquer the demons of the past and shine brighter than ever before.

And sometimes, just sometimes, these rekindled romances teach us a valuable lesson about the power of forgiveness, growth, and the resilience of love. Set aside egos, put being right to the side, and admit mistakes. They remind us that even when a love story seems to have reached its final chapter, there's always room for a sequel, a chance to rewrite the ending, and a hope for a happily ever after.

STRAIGHT from Safaree...

When a high-profile couple rekindles their romance, it's a journey that resonates deeply with me, having been in similar shoes.

The world watches as celebrities, who once publicly parted ways amidst a storm of media attention, venture into the arduous territory of trying it again. It's a spectacle that often leaves us wondering: Can they make it work this time? Have they learned from the mistakes and heartaches of their past, or are they merely walking down the same path that led to their first breakup?

The decision to reignite the flame to give love a second chance in the unforgiving glare of the spotlight is not for the faint of heart. It's a choice laden with complexities and more questions from others and sometimes ourselves. Can they rebuild the trust that may have been shattered? Have they grown individually and as a couple? And perhaps most importantly, can they navigate the pressures and expectations of the public eye? We may not have it all figured out but we know it's worth a shot.

Rekindling a romance, especially in the bright spotlight, is like embarking on an emotional rollercoaster. It's a journey I can attest to, filled with hurdles and victories, demons to confront, and ultimately, an incredible sense of enlightenment and emotional clarity.

When we give love another shot, it's often met with both curiosity and skepticism from the public. People wonder if the lessons have been learned, if the wounds have healed, and if the past can genuinely be put behind. It's a journey that requires a great deal of soul-searching and self-improvement.

For me, rekindling a romance meant diving headfirst into a whirlwind of emotions. It meant confronting my own demons, those inner struggles and past mistakes that contributed to the initial breakup. It wasn't always easy, and there were moments of doubt and fear. It involved addressing the issues that had plagued the relationship, whether it was communication, trust, or personal growth. It meant having those tough conversations, clearing the air of lingering doubts, and working together to create a healthier, more sustainable partnership. But the desire to make it work, to rebuild a once strong connection, was a driving force.

Confronting those inner demons, whether they were personal insecurities or past relationship patterns, was perhaps the most enlightening part of this journey. It meant acknowledging areas where I needed to grow and change, not just for the relationship but for my own personal development.

As the path unfolded, and as we put in the effort to rebuild what was once lost, there was an incredible sense of clarity and emotional liberation. It's like lifting a weight off your shoulders, knowing that you've faced your fears, learned from your mistakes, and emerged stronger on the other side.

CHAPTER TWELVE

Love Beyond the Lens: Finding a Connection Amidst the Chaos

In a world where superstars dominate the headlines, there's something enchanting about love that transcends the boundaries of celebrity. It's a narrative that speaks to the heart, reminding us that genuine connections can be found in the most unexpected places, far from the blinding spotlight.

For celebrities, the path to finding love can be a treacherous one. The scrutiny, the expectations, and the constant media attention can make it challenging to establish authentic connections. Even encountering a person with genuine intentions and seeking something real can be scarce. That's why some have sought solace and companionship in the arms of non-celebrity partners. It's a deliberate step away from the frenzy of fame, a chance to experience quiet and private moments amidst the chaos.

The decision to link with someone outside the spotlight often serves as a shield against the relentless scrutiny that surrounds celebrity relationships. Instead of two stars coming together in a blaze of publicity, it's a more subdued affair. This quieter approach can bring a semblance of peace to an otherwise chaotic lifestyle, allowing for genuine moments of connection away from the prying eyes of the world.

The struggle for a celebrity to find love and a genuine connection with another person, famous or not, remains a constant challenge. It's a reminder that amidst the glamour, the wealth, and the fame, what matters is the authenticity of the bond between two people. Love beyond fame is a testament to the enduring power of human connection, proving that no matter who you are, love knows no bounds.

Navigating the Challenges of Dating Outside of Fame

One of the most profound challenges that can arise when a celebrity dates someone other than a famous person is the need for the non-celebrity partner to feel secure. When your loved one is constantly in the public eye, receiving adoration, attention, and sometimes even adulation, it can be a daunting experience. The celebrity partner might grapple with feelings of inadequacy or jealousy. It takes patience and understanding to navigate these emotions. Establishing trust and open communication is key in overcoming this hurdle.

Understanding schedules is another crucial part of these relationships. Celebrities often have demanding and unpredictable timetables due to their work in the entertainment industry. This means missed dinners, canceled plans, and moments of solitude for their partners. The celebrity partner needs to be adaptable and patient, recognizing that the red carpet and late-night shoots are part of the celebrity's life. This is often difficult, as in other relationships they could've been the more esteemed, so this new lifestyle takes some getting used to. It also requires honesty about its effects and how it is affecting both people, with a need for check-ins to be planned.

Comprehending the unique personality traits that often come with celebrities is essential. The intense drive, ambition, and determination required to succeed in the spotlight can sometimes translate into strong-willed or perfectionist personalities. It's important for both partners to appreciate these qualities and harmonize them within the relationship, not villainize or weaponize them.

Celebrities endure immense pressure from the public and the industry, which can take a toll on their mental wellbeing. They must often develop a thick skin to withstand constant scrutiny and criticism. For their partners, understanding this mental toughness and providing emotional support when needed can be a profound way to contribute to a healthy relationship.

The non-celebrity partner might find they are thrust into a world of fame and glamour they never expected. This sudden exposure to the media and paparazzi can be overwhelming. It's crucial to discuss boundaries, privacy, and how to handle public attention as a couple.

While these challenges are undoubtedly present, they don't overshadow the beauty of love beyond fame. With mutual respect, open communication, and a deep connection, relationships between a celebrity and non-celebrity can thrive. They serve as a reminder that, despite the complexities of fame, love is a universal force that transcends all boundaries.

STRAIGHT from Safaree...

I've discovered that finding genuine connections with non-famous individuals can be both a challenge and a breath of fresh air. When you're in the public eye, it's no secret that some people might be drawn to you for the wrong reasons – whether it's fame, fortune, or a taste of the glamorous lifestyle. But amidst the chaos and uncertainty, there's a beauty in discovering authenticity amidst the crowd.

One thing I've learned is these connections can sprout from the most unexpected places. It could be through social media, where a simple message or comment can lead to meaningful conversations. It might happen at parties, where you meet someone who sees beyond the celebrity facade and connects with you on a personal level. Even the unlikeliest of places, like strip clubs or encounters with fans at my events, have led to genuine connections. Sometimes it's as simple as a friend of a friend introducing you to someone who understands you in ways you never imagined.

However, it's not all sunshine and rainbows. Personal challenges come with these connections. The stress and worry can be overwhelming. It's natural to question whether someone is genuinely interested in you or if they're after the perks that come with your fame. It keeps you on your toes, and it's tough to let your guard down.

Safety becomes a paramount concern. When you meet someone randomly, especially through the chaotic environment of an event or party, there's always that element of unpredictability. Trusting a stranger with your heart can be daunting, and you need to be cautious.

But despite these challenges, when you find that genuine connection, it's like discovering a hidden gem. The ability to connect with someone who values you for who you are, beyond the fame and fortune, is an incredible feeling. It reminds you that love knows no boundaries and can blossom in the most unexpected places.

So while the journey of love beyond fame might have its twists and turns, the destination is worth every moment of uncertainty. It's a testament to the resilience of the human heart and the beauty of genuine connections that can be found amidst the chaos of this world.

CHAPTER THIRTEEN

Life After Love

When the glitz and glamour of celebrity relationships are not taking center stage, equally significant but less talked about is life after love. When the world watches your romantic journey with anticipation, it's overwhelming to face the aftermath of a fizzled high-profile relationship. Yet this is the phase where true self-discovery, growth, and self-worth can flourish.

Moving on from a celebrity relationship can be as challenging as it is liberating. When two public figures part ways, it's often done amidst a flurry of media attention and public scrutiny. Every detail of the breakup is dissected, every emotion is analyzed, and every step forward is tracked. The pressure to heal and move on can feel insurmountable. Whether the lovelorn were ready or not, putting on a brave face and living life on their own terms is important. "Fake it until you make it" becomes the path forward.

But during these moments of transition actual personal growth begins. Rediscovering self-worth is a crucial part of life after love. In the spotlight, it's easy to get caught up in the identity defined by the relationship. Who you are as an individual can become intertwined with the persona of the couple. As the relationship dissolves, there's an opportunity to reclaim your sense of self, or even rethink it. It's about finding value within, recognizing your strengths, and understanding that your worth isn't defined by your relationship status or by anyone else. This journey often involves introspection, self-care, and reconnecting with passions and interests that may have taken a backseat during the relationship.

One of the most significant challenges is learning to redefine your identity outside of the public eye. When the world is accustomed to seeing you as part of a famous couple, stepping into your own spotlight can be intimidating. But it's also a chance to rewrite your narrative, pursue personal goals, and embrace a newfound sense of independence.

In addition, life after love offers an opportunity to reflect on the lessons learned from the past relationship. What went wrong, what you've discovered about yourself, and what you want in your next Chapter of love all become crucial considerations. It's a period of growth, both emotionally and mentally, that can ultimately lead to healthier, more fulfilling relationships.

One of the most exhilarating aspects of life after love is the newfound freedom to have fun without constraints. You're no longer bound by the expectations and responsibilities of a relationship. This often translates into unforgettable nights out, spontaneous adventures, and an overall sense of light-heartedness. Whether it's dancing the night away with friends, embarking on spontaneous road trips, or trying thrilling activities you've never considered before, this phase is all about having fun and relishing every moment.

Parties and social gatherings become opportunities to reconnect with old friends and make new ones. It's a chance to expand your social circle, meet people from different walks of life, and enjoy the diversity of human connections. In these moments, you rediscover the joy of camaraderie and the simple pleasures of laughter and shared experiences.

Eventually, dating again may become a thrilling prospect. You're no longer limited to one romantic partner, and this newfound freedom lets you explore various connections. It's a time to meet interesting individuals, discover common interests, and appreciate the spectrum of personalities and perspectives. Each date offers a chance to learn more about yourself and what you seek in a partner.

Exploring the world takes on a new dimension. Solo travel or adventures with friends can be enriching experiences. It's a time to immerse yourself in different cultures, savor exotic cuisines, and create memories that are uniquely yours. Traveling becomes a form of self-discovery, letting you understand your own desires and aspirations on a deeper level.

Creating new experiences becomes a way to rebuild your sense of self and the identity you choose. Whether it's pursuing passions unfulfilled, taking up new hobbies, or setting ambitious goals, this phase is about personal growth and self-improvement. You have the time and freedom to invest in yourself, nurturing your talents and ambitions.

Life after a love breakup offers a sense of unparalleled liberation, bursting with adventure, self-exploration, and the invigoration of fresh beginnings. Though a breakup may signify the end of one love story, it simultaneously serves as the prologue to the next thrilling Chapter in your life. Embrace it wholeheartedly, savor the freedom to rediscover your authentic self, and explore what genuinely brings you happiness. This journey, which resonates with individuals, whether celebrities or not, is all about healing, self-discovery, and relentlessly pursuing personal growth. While the public may be fixated on the spectacle of high-profile breakups, the inner metamorphosis genuinely characterizes this Chapter of your life. It stands as a testament to the enduring strength of the human spirit and its boundless capacity for personal growth, whether one lives in the spotlight or behind the scenes.

STRAIGHT from Safaree...

Life after love has been an exhilarating journey, filled with incredible parties, passionate connections, and wild adventures that defy the ordinary. Stepping away from the spotlight of a high-profile relationship and being removed from under that microscope unleashed a wave of electrifying experiences. I'm here to take you along for this thrilling ride.

Picture this: regular nights that transformed into epic adventures, where laughter and music set the world on fire, and every party felt like it could go on forever. These were the times where every event was a masterpiece, and champagne was almost raining from the skies.

In this whirlwind, incredible women became part of this journey, each one a magnetic force of nature. Every encounter was like a scene from a movie, filled with passion and energy that leaves you breathless.

Jet-setting became my way of life; one exotic location effortlessly transitioned into another. It was a life lived out of a suitcase, where every day brought new adventures and new companions who added their own electrifying spark to the experience.

And then there was the pure joy of switching hotels, like changing costumes in this grand theater of life. Each hotel had its own story to tell, from exploration to savoring exotic cuisines. These were the moments that made life feel surreal.

In this wild and passionate journey, there was also profound healing and personal reinvention. It was a journey of growth, a chance to redefine priorities, and a realization of the incredible power of self-worth. It was about finding happiness from within, a reminder that no amount of fame or fortune could match the sheer joy of authenticity.

I hope you can feel the intense passion, the wild energy, and the sheer thrill that pulses through when looking at my life. It's a reminder that even after heartbreak, there's a world of adventures and opportunities waiting to be seized. It's a journey of rediscovery, reinvention, and pursuing happiness.

CHAPTER FOURTEEN

Lessons from the Stars

Celebrity relationships often play out like modern-day fairy tales, complete with dazzling events, red carpet appearances, and intense media coverage. Yet beyond the glitz and glamour, there are valuable lessons to be gleaned from the romantic escapades of the stars. Whether you're navigating love as a public figure or simply seeking insights into the complexities of modern relationships, these takeaways from celebrity dating experiences offer invaluable advice on balancing love, fame, and privacy.

One of the most striking lessons from celebrities is the importance of authenticity. In an age of carefully curated images and public personas, genuine connections stand out. Stars who are unapologetically themselves often find more enduring love amidst the spotlight and can maintain a lifestyle that can be appreciated.

Balancing public life and personal privacy is an art form. Celebrities often teach us that while sharing aspects of a relationship can be endearing, it's equally crucial to preserve moments just for you and your partner. When everything is staged or for show, you start to question if anything is real, which can affect the sustainability of the partnership.

Effective communication is the cornerstone of any successful relationship. But in the celebrity world, where schedules are hectic and distances can be vast, it's essential. When layering on the onset temptations and constant interactions with other beautiful people, the celebrity lifestyle brings unique challenges that can only be navigated by healthy communication. Learning to speak openly and honestly is a lesson we can all take to heart, but it is especially important in celebrity relationships.

Being in the public eye often means dealing with criticism. Learning to weather the storm and not let negativity affect your relationship is a skill worth mastering. Rejecting discouraging opinions and false narratives must also become a new skill. Otherwise, things can get toxic.

In demanding careers, nurturing one's mental and emotional well-being is essential. It's a reminder that taking care of yourself lets you be a better partner. You cannot bring your best self to a relationship if you are never the focus, so take time to work on your personal goals and desires to be the best partner you can be.

Relationships, like life, are constantly changing. Learning to adapt and grow with your partner, rather than against them, is a lesson that resonates with many celebrities who have weathered the ups and downs of fame and love.

Having a support system is vital. Celebrities often turn to close friends, family, or therapists to help navigate the unique challenges that come with their relationships. Seeking advice and support when needed is a sign of strength.

Recognizing red flags early is crucial. Celebrities, like anyone else, have experienced toxic relationships, and their stories serve as cautionary tales for us all. Trust your instincts and focus on your health.

Perhaps one of the most heartening lessons is that love can be found in unexpected places. Whether it's with a fellow celebrity, a childhood friend, or someone from a different walk of life, love knows no bounds.

Finally, remaining true to your values, desires, and boundaries is paramount. Celebrities who have found lasting love often credit this to their authenticity and an unwavering commitment to their own happiness.

The romantic journeys of celebrities offer not only entertainment but also valuable insights into the complexities of modern love. Whether you're in the spotlight or simply seeking love in your own way, these lessons from the stars serve as a guiding light in navigating the intricate tapestry of relationships, fame, and personal growth.

CHAPTER FIFTEEN

Dating and New Money

When dating with new money, love takes on an exhilarating dimension, and every moment shimmers with riches and excitement.

Imagine the mindset of celebrities who ascended to a life where the extraordinary is the new normal. They step into a world where desires know no limits and where the world becomes their playground. It's akin to living in a perpetual dream, where every wish is at their fingertips and the possibilities are as vast as the universe itself.

One of the most striking parts of dating with new money is the ability to craft an image that's nothing short of spectacular. With wealth flowing like a river, celebrities can transform themselves into paragons of style and elegance. They have the means to adorn themselves in attire that not only captivates but also mirrors their newfound status as icons of prosperity.

In this world of opulence, dating becomes a thrilling odyssey beyond imagination. It's a place where grand experiences aren't just occasional luxuries; they are everyday occurrences: Think Michelin-starred restaurants, private dining under the stars, and globe-trotting escapades with private jets and luxury yachts that unlock doors to the world's most exclusive destinations.

But the intrigue doesn't stop there. Potential partners aren't simply attracted to the wealth; they are irresistibly drawn to the aura of glamour and triumph that surrounds these celebrities. The enchantment of being near someone who seemingly holds the world in their hands exudes an undeniable allure, creating an intoxicating and magnetic force.

However, we must unveil the complex layers beneath the surface. The line between authentic affection and attraction to the extravagant lifestyle blurs, leaving us to ponder: Can love flourish in the radiant glow of immense wealth and fame? Are these relationships crafted for lasting connection, or are they as fleeting as a shooting star? This is the issue that plagues celebrities as they come into their own and become stars. It's a struggle to know who is there for the right reasons, or who is hitching their wagon onto a moving target.

Maybe it's time to shed light on these ideas through a vivid example. This real-life scenario exemplifies the profound influence that newfound wealth can wield over the dating experiences of a rising young celebrity.

For example:

In mid-2000, a young superstar who had captured the nation's heart found himself at the threshold of stardom. His first hit single had climbed the charts, and with it came a life-changing moment: receiving his first million-dollar paycheck. At this point in his early twenties, this young superstar was riding high on a wave of success that had propelled him into the music industry's elite.

The moment he held that million-dollar check, a rush of emotions surged through him. Excitement, pride, and the weight of new-found responsibility all mingled in his mind. He realized that his life was about to change in ways he could hardly imagine. This was validation for the years of hard work and dedication he had poured into his craft.

In the realm of dating, this young superstar was no longer the un-known talent striving to make it big. He had become a heartthrob, with an ever-growing fan base of admirers. His boyish charm, incredible stage presence, and magnetic charisma made him ir-resistible to many. The allure of celebrity dating was undeniable, with opportunities to meet fellow stars and explore romantic con-nections at every turn.

However, this young superstar's dating life wasn't all glitz and glamour. His career was skyrocketing, and it left him with a packed schedule. Recording sessions, world tours, and promotional events consumed much of his time. Balancing a burgeoning music career with personal relationships proved challenging. While he longed for moments of normalcy and the chance to nurture con-nections, the demands of his profession often took precedence.

As the years rolled on, this young superstar continued to achieve greater success and faced the highs and lows that fame brought. His dating life, marked by fleeting connections and intense public scrutiny, reflected the complex and often turbulent world of celeb-rity romance.

Beneath the surface, the line between authentic affection and attraction to extravagance blurs. As we've seen in our example, pursuing fame and fortune can both empower and complicate personal relationships. It's a world where dreams materialize, but the demanding spotlight of celebrity can cast shadows over the path to lasting love. So as the final curtain falls on this captivating exploration, we're left with the age-old question: Is love in the radiant glow of immense wealth and fame destined for eternity, or is it as fleeting as a shooting star?

CHAPTER SIXTEEN

A Moment for Life: When Fantasy and Reality Collide

In the world of untamed desires and starry infatuations, there exists a temptation like no other: In lieu of dating or being in a relationship with a star, going for the ride of a lifetime and sharing a single night, a fleeting encounter, with a celebrity crush. It's a provocative fantasy that ignites the imagination, quickens the pulse, and fuels the senses. But this captivating notion isn't limited to the glitz and glamour of the famous interacting with one another; everyday people, too, have savored moments with their celebrity idols. In this chapter, we plunge into the intoxicating allure of "A Moment for Life," exploring the fervent desires and passionate fantasies that awaken when sex meets fame, for both celebrities and starry-eyed dreamers.

It all begins innocently enough—a chance glimpse of their favorite celebrity on a magazine cover, a music video that leaves them spellbound, or a mesmerizing performance under the spotlight. Celebrities, like regular folks, find themselves ensnared by the charm, talent, and charisma of a particular star. Their allure becomes a beacon of fascination, something that beckons them closer, whether they admit it or not. It's the inception of a dream, a fantasy that takes root and refuses to let go.

As the fantasy deepens, they can't help but imagine what it would be like to share a night with their celebrity crush. These day-dreams unfold like scenes from a Hollywood romance: a chance encounter at a lavish event, a stolen moment in the soft glow of candlelight, or an invite to an exclusive after-party. Though these dreams may never materialize, they bring an electrifying sense of passion and longing.

Anticipation is a potent mix of nerves and exhilaration. It's the thrill of seeing that familiar face in the flesh, of experiencing their infectious smile and the warmth of their presence. Every moment leading to this potential encounter is charged with longing and desire. They envision the words they might exchange, the laughter that could fill the air, and the secrets they could share.

But "A Moment for Life" isn't limited to the realm of fantasy; it's about pushing the boundaries of possibility, potentially seizing the fantasy when finding yourself in the right place at the right time. We explore the sexiness that surrounds a passionate encounter that becomes legendary, both for the celebrity and everyday dreamer.

Yet as the sun rises on our fantasies, the morning after often carries a bittersweet reminder. "A Moment for Life" may become a cherished memory, but it also underscores the reality that desires are woven into the fabric of time and circumstance. Celebrities and everyday people ponder the implications of sharing an intimate rendezvous with someone who exists in the spotlight, whose life is a tapestry of fame and fortune.

This is more than a mere fantasy; it's a celebration of the enduring allure of what could be, of desire and possibly even love. It's a tribute to those heart-pounding instances when the line between reality and fantasy blurs. It's an acknowledgment that in the world of unfettered dreams, anything is possible—even if only for a moment. Embark on a journey through the captivating realm of passion and fantasy, where there remains an intoxicating promise that lingers in the hearts of dreamers, romantics, celebrities, and everyday people.

Sometimes, the Jane Doe, no-nonsense baddie with an unconventional background embarks on this journey and lands the chance occurrence of a stolen night, and maybe even surprises with her exceptional skills. Hailing from a world far removed from the glitz and glamour of high-end luxuries, she might not boast the same refined lifestyle as the world's most celebrated celebrities but has a hunger for more that drives the moment further. Instead, she brings her confident and unique flair to the table, creating an experience that's a little rough around the edges but unforgettable, nonetheless. As she refuses to be ignored and grabs his attention, both realize this is a time where anything goes and they both feel so alive, which electrifies the moment.

In this highly anticipated moment her entire body becomes an instrument, moving with a grace and precision that transcends anything Hollywood could fabricate. Her motions flow seamlessly, guided by an intuitive knowledge of the body's needs. Engaging in sex with a celebrity can be an invigorating phenomenon that involves both the body and mind of each person. When lovers take to the bed their bodies are aroused, igniting a deep sense of desire and vitality. The sensation of perspiration sliding down their bodies is a gift to the lovers pushing each other to the pinnacle of their limits. With expectations of pleasure, and sometimes pain, they dominate one another into the ultimate climax if both can submit and give in to the moment.

The experience is an adventure and undeniably euphoric. With each masterful movement, she weaves her unique brand of magic, effortlessly transporting them from the contrived celebrity landscape to a realm where they're on top of the world. Everyday social media models and around the way baddies have nothing to lose and leave it all in the experience. With nothing to prove, ignoring her insecurities and enjoying the real effect she has on this person that seemed so untouchable makes it all even more extraordinary.

STRAIGHT from Safaree...

Yo, I gotta keep it a hundred; as I'm on this journey down memory lane, I can't forget about the wild proposals and one-night adventures that have made their way into my life. It's wild, and you know what? It's kinda flattering, to be honest. The idea that someone wants to get close to me just to experience what it'd be like—that's something else, man.

But here's the deal – all that glitters ain't gold. Sometimes it's the simplest and most authentic connections that shine the brightest. Believe it or not, physical chemistry and sexual prowess ain't locked in with the most famous celebrities. In fact, I've chopped it up with my close friends and we've come to the conclusion that it's often the opposite.

Those who don't have to deal with the whole celebrity status thing or the insecurities that can come with being a mega starlet are the ones who bring a unique kind of excitement to these encounters. These less famous folks—some folks even call 'em "ordinary baddies"—they're the real deal, man. They create moments that stick in your memory, and these encounters often turn into cherished memories for both sides.

There's something about these connections: no need to put on a front, no pressure to maintain an image. It's in these low-key, down-to-earth moments that you find that true chemistry, that authenticity, and a connection that's just real and uninhibited.

While the world's all about the glitz and glamour, don't forget that beneath all that, when the spotlight's not so bright, there's a whole world of magic and authenticity just waiting to be discovered. It's in the arms of someone whose stardom comes from the heart, from being true to themselves. So keep it real, stay true to yourself, and appreciate those simple, authentic moments in life. That's where the real allure is—you know what I'm saying?

CHAPTER SEVENTEEN

Allure of the Barbie

Dating the ultimate Barbie—man, it was something else. She brought a whole lot of excitement and glamour to my life, and let me tell you, it was like stepping into a world of extravagance that I never knew existed. But here's the thing: It also came with a headache that I loved to hate.

Let's talk shopping habits – she could shop up a storm. It was like retail therapy on steroids, and I couldn't help but be impressed by her sheer dedication to style. Every outing became a full-blown fashion show, and my front-row seat felt like an everlasting shopping spree, moments stretching into what felt like eternity.

And the bratty behavior—well, it was all part of the package. She knew how to turn on the charm when she wanted something, and it was hard to resist. I might have found myself wrapped around her little finger, but I wasn't complaining because it came with those moments of pure Aquafina bliss.

But it wasn't all sunshine and roses. My ultimate Barbie could be stubborn as all get-out. Once she made up her mind, I might as well have been talking to a brick wall. It led to some epic battles, but you know what? It also added a whole lot of spice to the relationship. It was like a rollercoaster I couldn't resist, even though it gave me a headache now and then.

Dating someone like the ultimate Barbie felt like living in a fantasy world. I got the highs, the lows, and everything in between. It was an adventure, man, and I couldn't help but love every moment of it. It was like being thrown into the most exciting show on Earth, and we were the stars. Every day felt like a magical journey, complete with all the ups and downs that came with it.

For those considering dating a Barbie, here's a piece of advice: Embrace the adventure and enjoy the ride. Be prepared for exciting moments, occasional challenges, and lots of laughter. Understand that she's a high-spirited individual with quirks and a tendency to go on shopping sprees like nothing you've ever seen. So appreciate the charm and positivity she brings into your life and remember that the occasional stubbornness only adds spice to the relationship.

For the Barbies out there, here's a tip: Embrace your unique charm and magnetic personality. You bring joy wherever you go, and your energy is infectious. Don't be afraid to be high maintenance at times; it's all part of your allure. Just remember to appreciate the men who embark on this rollercoaster journey with you and let them in on the magic you bring to life. In the end, love, laughter, and shared experiences are what make your journey truly remarkable.

Tale of Triumph:
From Unsung Hero to Celestial Titan

STRAIGHT from Safaree...

Yo, let me take you through this wild ride. It all started when I teamed up with a Mega Starlet. Looked like some modern fairy tale from the outside, right? We're talking about a life of insane shopping, yachts that skimmed pristine waters, and hotels fancier than some palaces. But let me peel back the layers, and you'll see there's more to this story.

Picture this: Me and the Starlet, a modern Cinderella and Prince Charming. We owned those red carpets; our fashion game was off the charts. Hotels? Regal doesn't even cover it. We enjoyed city views that'd make your jaw drop, and room service menus that read like gourmet symphonies.

Even more riveting than the superficial was what lay beneath: the love we shared. Our bond meant more than words can express. "Best friends" was an understatement, "longtime lovers" a trivialization. Simply put, we were just us. And no one truly understood that or got that except us.

Now here is the twist. Behind all the glitz, I was an unsung hero, a creative genius building an empire in the background. While everyone was busy gushing over her fame, my talents and charisma were the real deal. I was a driving force, a brilliant mind lurking in the shadows of that blinding spotlight.

But hold on—as you can imagine, there was drama emerging to upend everything. Under the fancy paper and pink bows, the Starlet was not the gift she seemed to be. That sizzling chemistry became more like smoke and mirrors. Eventually lies, betrayal, and infidelity cast a dark cloud over our narrative.

Our relationship, the fun, the authenticity all turned into what looked like a business deal. Former lovers assumed roles of employer and employee. Our interactions lost their spark, our physical connection became stale, and our talks became more argumentative and disrespectful.

I found myself in a tight spot, love under siege. Our once-unbreakable bond was cracking: sharp attacks, growing disconnection, indifference, toxicity, false accusations, and harm like a storm. When love clashes with your well-being, you know it's time to move on.

The craziest part is that while grieving a love and life lost, I also had to fight for my life. I faced the risk of being blacklisted, scandal-dragged, and scorned by an industry I deeply influenced. Though this was my rock bottom moment, I rose from the mud with unwavering resilience, like a phoenix. Guided by a fearless ally, a titan amongst gods, I became a superstar. I stepped into my own light and was able to shine.

Through this crazy ride, the paparazzi played their role, capturing the highs, the lows, the glam, and the scandals. They were both friends and foes, casting shadows on our love while pushing us to superstardom.

My journey was a wild dive into the intricacies of celebrity dating. It's a story that goes beyond the glitz, showing my indomitable spirit, charisma, and resilience. This is a tale of triumph against all odds, where the hero rises from the mud and scandal to celestial heights as a celebrity titan, rewriting his destiny.

Sure, dating a celeb is glamorous, but it's also loaded with drama, heartbreak and deception. Behind the allure, there's vulnerability and challenges, a complex reality hiding behind fame.

CHAPTER EIGHTEEN

Celebrity Dating Styles Unveiled

While dating in ordinary life can take many forms, for a celebrity it can be described in three unique approaches, because they unfold amidst fame's spotlight. These dating styles defy conventions and provide valuable insights into how celebrities navigate their dating lives. First, we encounter The Monogamy Enthusiast, champions of committed dating in a world often associated with casual flings. Then we step into the world of The Passion Pioneers, celebrities who openly embrace dating, focusing on honesty and trust. Finally, we join The Nomadic Lover, free spirits seeking dating adventures without borders, transcending cultural boundaries. These approaches paint a vivid picture of the rich tapestry of celebrity dating, showing that dating in the limelight can be a diverse and fascinating adventure.

The Monogamy Enthusiast

Celebrity relationships often seem as short-lived as the flash of paparazzi cameras, but a select few stand out, like *The Monogamy*

Enthusiast. These celebrities, in their resolute commitment to traditional relationships, defy the prevailing norms of flings and open affairs so often linked to fame. They're the torchbearers of enduring love, and beneath the surface of Hollywood's glitz, their stories are nothing short of captivating.

Within the echo chambers of Hollywood, where gossip columns thrive on tales of short-lived romances, *The Monogamy Enthusiast* radiates a different aura. They don't bow to the temptation of fleeting connections; instead, they embrace the profound beauty of commitment. For them, love isn't a passing phase; it's a testament to the enduring power of human connection.

Their relationships shatter stereotypes. These celebrities boldly challenge the notion that fame and promiscuity go hand-in-hand. They serve as beacons, illuminating a path where love, loyalty, and monogamy are celebrated, not overlooked. Their choices echo in the hearts of fans, reminding the world that enduring love is possible, even in the brightest of spotlights.

Behind the facade of red carpets and camera flashes, *The Monogamy Enthusiast* leads a life far from the ordinary. They navigate a world filled with extravagant parties and seductive temptations. The pressure to conform to the industry's norms is relentless, and the media's watchful eye scrutinizes their every move.

In this glamorous yet challenging world, this couple often finds solace in each other. Their love becomes a fortress, a sanctuary against the clamor of the outside world. It's a delicate dance, where their commitment serves as both armor and refuge. They face moments of doubt and temptation, but their love for one another, deep-rooted and unwavering, is their guiding light.

And then there are those enchanting moments when one of them makes their love official beneath the shimmering Hollywood lights. Picture this: a starlit evening, perhaps on a moonlit beach or an opulent rooftop, where the world seems to hold its breath. The proposal is a symphony of emotions, a crescendo of love and commitment that resonates through the Hollywood Hills.

Amidst the twinkling stars, with the city of angels as their witness, one of them gets down on bended knee, offering a ring that shines as brightly as their love. It's a moment of pure magic, a scene straight out of a fairytale, reminding us that even in the most extraordinary of circumstances, love can be both timeless and enchanting.

The Monogamy Enthusiasts have written their love stories with ink that refuses to fade. Theirs is a narrative of unwavering commitment, a defiance of Hollywood's transient romances that offers moments of pure, heartfelt enchantment beneath the stars.

The Passion Pioneers

Within celebrity dating, a unique breed emerges – *The Passion Pioneers*. They are bold forerunners of love, fearlessly challenging conventions in a world where relationships are often hidden behind closed doors. These celebrities, amidst the glamour and flashbulbs, are the ones who courageously and openly embrace love in the public eye.

The lives of *The Passion Pioneers* are a riveting dive into the extraordinary. They defy the conventions of traditional monogamy, proudly displaying their relationships to the world. Their love stories unfold amidst the cameras, unfiltered and without reservation. They stand apart, a testament to their audacious commitment to living life on their own terms, where love knows no bounds.

Amidst the tumultuous sea of celebrity dating, these trailblazers focus on something often overlooked: honest communication and consent. In a world where tabloids sensationalize every connection, they rise above the noise. Their relationships are built on trust, mutual understanding, and the unwavering belief that love thrives when unburdened by pretense.

Their love is not limited to hushed whispers or hidden glances. Instead, they throw open the doors to unforgettable nights, where opulence intertwines with the boundless potential of love in the glitzy world of fame. These gatherings are not mere parties; they are extravagant declarations of love's vibrancy. They celebrate passion, companionship, and the exhilarating journey of love without restraint.

The Passion Pioneers redefine what it means to be a celebrity in love. They shatter the conventional mold, proving that love can be a thrilling adventure without constraints, even amidst the dazzling world of fame. Their relationships are not just stories; they are living proof that genuine connections triumph over societal norms.

The Passion Pioneers are the torchbearers of love, fearlessly unveiling their relationships in a world that often hides them away.

They illuminate a path where love is an exhilarating journey, unfiltcred and unapologetic, daring the world to embrace its many shades and intricacies.

The Nomadic Lover

These stars live a life of freedom, dating in multiple cities and embracing adventures without borders. Imagine a life where you hop from one city to another, exploring love without being tied down. These celebs don't limit themselves to one place. From New York's bright lights to Rio de Janeiro's sultry charm, their love story is a tale of curiosity and a hunger for new experiences.

The Nomadic Lover's mindset is all about freedom. They don't follow conventional relationship rules. Instead, they thrive on new connections and the unpredictable nature of love. For them, love is a journey of self-discovery, always evolving. For a *Celebrity Nomadic Lover*, love isn't static; it's an ever-changing landscape. They cherish diverse human connections and embrace spontaneity. Late-night adventures, exciting encounters, and wild escapades are part of their lives.

At the core of the *Nomadic Lover* is a love story in pursuit of freedom. They love without restraint, explore without limits, and break free from societal norms. Their love, like their lifestyle, is about living life on their terms.

For *Nomadic Lovers*, love knows no boundaries, and life is an ever-evolving adventure. It's a bold existence that challenges the norm, where love is not confined but celebrated as a thrilling journey of the heart.

This exploration of celebrity dating has unveiled three unconventional dating approaches that defy norms and paint a vivid picture of how dating unfolds within the glitzy world of fame, from *The Monogamy Enthusiast*, who stands as a symbol of committed dating in a realm often associated with casual encounters, to the *Passion Pioneers*, who openly embrace dating with honesty and trust, and finally, to *The Nomadic Lovers*, who venture across borders in their pursuit of connections, challenging societal norms.

These descriptions collectively show dating in the celebrity sphere takes on diverse forms, each representing a unique path to connection. They highlight the resilience and audacity of dating amidst the ever-evolving world of fame, showcasing that in matters of the heart, diversity thrives in the limelight.

CHAPTER NINETEEN

The Star-Studded Path to Personal Development

In celebrity romance, where love and fame become intertwined, an insatiable hunger for personal growth and development takes center stage. In this arena, love stories, filled with passion or marked by turbulence, play out for the entire world to witness beneath the relentless spotlight.

Now visualize this: Two entertainment titans, both driven by ambition and bound by creative vision, collide in a grand display of talent. However, when their ambitions and egos clash, what was once a symbol of creative promise undergoes a transformation, erupting into a fiery and highly publicized breakup. Tempers flare, grievances mount, and the battleground extends to the expansive realm of social media.

Here, X (formerly known as Twitter) clashes, Instagram tirades, and incomprehensible posts become their chosen battleground, where they share their grievances for the world to witness. An audience, captivated by the drama, watches with bated breath as speculation, rumors, and relentless scrutiny follow. Every word, every gesture is dissected, and what was once a private dispute evolves into a global spectacle, ensnaring millions in its whirlwind of controversy.

For these celebrities, the repercussions are widespread. Their reputations teeter on the brink, endorsements vanish like a fleeting illusion, and professional prospects crumble. Yet, amid this whirlwind, beneath the dramatic facade, lives an indisputable truth—a need for personal growth.

In the high-stakes theater of their lives, personal growth isn't a luxury; it's a lifeline. It empowers them with emotional resilience, fortifies their self-esteem, and bestows the invaluable gift of effective communication—a vital defense against the relentless scrutiny of celebrity.

Celebrities tussle with the unrelenting public eye, where every facet of their lives undergoes ceaseless judgment. Personal growth becomes their refuge, an internal strengthening to withstand even the most ferocious storms of public opinion.

The unique challenges of celebrity relationships, encompassing demanding schedules, long-distance hurdles, and the alluring temptation of external influences, drive them toward emotional intelligence and self-improvement. Personal growth equips them with the tools to construct and nurture profound connections.

Most celebrities try to present themselves as perfect, which can lead to stress, anxiety, and a never-ending attempt to meet society's expectations. Personal growth gives them the inner strength to pursue happiness in their own way.

In the ups and downs in the world of fame, celebrities turn to personal growth techniques like therapy and self-reflection as their lifelines. These practices help them navigate the challenges and protect their mental health.

Many celebrities embrace their roles as an inspiration to others. Personal growth enables them not only to evolve as individuals but also to set an example of growth, motivating their fans and peers to embark on their own journeys of self-improvement.

Personal growth becomes the North Star in their journey through the challenging world of fame. It helps them stay true to themselves and build strong, meaningful relationships. In a world where love stories are watched closely by the public and where perfection is always sought after, personal growth shines as a guiding light for self-discovery and the foundation of lasting, genuine connections.

CHAPTER TWENTY

Navigating the Relentless Spotlight: Celebrity Relationships Under Scrutiny

Imagine being in a relationship where every move, every choice, and every heartfelt gesture is subjected to intense scrutiny by the ever-watchful public eye. The pressure to have a flawless image becomes an unending challenge, even for the most resilient individuals. In this section, we journey into the world of towering expectations, unrelenting standards, and relentless pursuit of perfection. We shed light on the profound toll celebrity takes on the emotional well-being of those who find themselves in the spotlight.

For celebrities, the weight of maintaining an impeccable image is all-encompassing and ceaseless. Their romantic lives, from grand romantic gestures to the most private moments, face unyielding scrutiny from both the media and the public. These groups' standards are often set impossibly high, demanding that these individuals consistently present themselves as the epitome of an ideal partner.

This relentless pursuit of perfection exacts a profound toll on their emotional well-being. It's as if they are trapped in a never-ending performance, perpetually onstage and under the microscope. The constant, haunting fear of making even the slightest misstep or revealing any vulnerability leads to moments of intense anxiety and self-doubt. The weight of these expectations often fosters a sense of isolation, where personal happiness takes a backseat to unrelenting efforts to meet the insurmountable standards dictated by the world.

The consequences of such immense pressure can be emotionally overwhelming. Many celebrities grapple with stress, anxiety, and even depression as they navigate the tumultuous waters of fame and relationships. These ceaseless expectations cast long and pervasive shadows over their lives, making it challenging to find solace in their personal connections.

Dating as a celebrity is nuanced and presents dramatic challenges. It's a world where the relentless quest for perfection casts enduring shadows over emotional well-being, pushing these luminaries to the precipice of personal sacrifice in their unwavering endeavor to meet the unattainable standards placed on them.

Understanding Celebrity Behavior

At the heart of this exploration is the recognition that celebrities, despite their larger-than-life personas, are human beings. They experience love, joy, heartbreak, and uncertainty like everyone else. However, their journey through the landscape of romance is colored by the extraordinary circumstances that fame gives to them.

One crucial facet of celebrity relationships is the relentless scrutiny under which they exist. Every move, every choice, and every expression of affection is analyzed, criticized, and celebrated by the public and the media. The pressure to have a flawless image, both individually and as a couple, can be suffocating. Thus their seemingly erratic dating choices often reflect a delicate balancing act between vulnerability and self-preservation.

Past traumas and betrayals, many of which have played out in the unforgiving spotlight of fame, significantly influence their approach to love. These experiences sow seeds of caution and mistrust, shaping their hesitancy to open their hearts to new partners. The glittering world they inhabit can be isolating, driving them to seek connections, even in unconventional ways.

As celebrities ascend higher on the ladder of fame, the weight of expectations becomes increasingly burdensome. The unrelenting demand for perfection in a society that idolizes physical appearance and scrutinizes choices can lead to bouts of insecurity and self-doubt. Their dating decisions may seem erratic when viewed from the outside.

Past heartbreaks, many of which are etched into the annals of celebrity gossip, leave indelible scars. These experiences leave a profound impact, influencing their ability to trust and commit to new relationships. The relentless pursuit of an ideal partner, driven by the fear of settling or making the same mistakes, often pushes them toward unconventional dating avenues.

Their exclusive social circles, populated by industry peers and fellow celebrities, further complicate matters. Relationships often intertwine with career ambitions, fostering complex dynamics where love and professional goals coexist. Deciphering the intricacies of celebrity behavior in relationships becomes an exploration of the human experience itself—a journey through the intricacies of desire, fear, and relentlessly pursuing connection.

In this quest to decode celebrity behavior in relationships, we unearth the hidden layers of their romantic lives. We gain insights into the emotional forces driving their choices, whether they seek solace in the spotlight or yearn for intimate moments away from the public eye. It's a journey of understanding that reveals the deeply human aspects of fame, where love and vulnerability transcend the boundaries of celebrity, offering a glimpse into the intricate web of their behavior in relationships.

Uncovering Hidden Trauma

As we delve more deeply into the intricacies of these romances, we find ourselves in complex narratives that involve betrayal, infidelity, abuse, and the haunting specter of childhood trauma.

Betrayal, in its many forms, is a haunting shadow that sometimes stretches its fingers into the lives of celebrities. The intense scrutiny they face can often exacerbate the consequences of betrayal, turning private moments of indiscretion into public spectacles. Trust, once broken, can be a fragile thing to mend, and the scars of betrayal can echo through relationships in unexpected ways, playing out on the public stage for all to see.

Infidelity, another specter that often looms in the background, doesn't discriminate between fame and obscurity. Celebrities, despite their public personas, are not immune to the temptations and complexities of romantic entanglements outside their primary relationships. The consequences of infidelity can be far-reaching, not only affecting the individuals involved but also casting a shadow over their public image, as the drama unfolds on television screens and in the pages of tabloids.

Abuse, a deeply distressing and often hidden facet of some celebrity relationships, leaves profound scars on the individuals involved. The power dynamics that fame can create sometimes exacerbate situations of abuse, making it even more challenging for victims to break free from toxic relationships. The consequences of abuse, whether physical or emotional, extend beyond the personal lives of celebrities, affecting their careers and overall well-being, sometimes becoming headlines.

Childhood trauma, often buried beneath layers of success and fame, can resurface in celebrity relationships. The wounds of the past, whether stemming from neglect, abuse, or abandonment, can influence the dynamics of their love lives. Some celebrities may seek to fill the emotional void left by childhood traumas through relationships, while others might grapple with deep-seated insecurities that manifest as trust issues or fear of intimacy, creating a compelling narrative in the public eye.

These intricate narratives of betrayal, infidelity, abuse, and childhood trauma become threads woven into the fabric of celebrity relationships. They add layers of complexity to the already challenging terrain of love in the public eye, and as these traumas play out on television screens and in their relationships, they become stories of vulnerability and resilience, where pursuing love often intersects with the scars of betrayal, infidelity, abuse, and the haunting echoes of childhood trauma.

When Untreated Trauma Hits the Big Screen

Under the unforgiving gaze of the public eye, a captivating saga unfolds. It's a journey deep into the hearts and minds of these larger-than-life figures, where past traumas and emotional baggage resurface in the most unexpected moments, often played out on the grand stage of national television.

Betrayal, infidelity, abuse, and childhood trauma emerge as the central themes of this gripping narrative. Betrayal takes center stage, as relationships face the shattering of trust, spotlighted before a global audience. Emotional confrontations, tearful apologies, and attempts at reconciliation become the raw material of talk shows and reality series, leaving audiences both spellbound and emotionally invested.

Infidelity adds a layer of scandal to the drama, with secret affairs and clandestine encounters exposed through paparazzi lenses and reality TV cameras. The emotional turmoil of those involved, from guilt-ridden confessions to defiant denials, plays out like a high-stakes melodrama, captivating viewers around the world.

Abuse, whether physical or emotional, casts a dark shadow, occasionally taking a shocking turn when instances of abuse are captured on camera or revealed in candid interviews. The media's role in addressing these issues comes into sharp focus, and the public demands justice as discussions about the industry's responsibility intensify.

Childhood trauma forms the backdrop for many celebrities and their struggles when these deep-seated wounds come to the forefront. Emotional scars from abandonment or abuse are exposed in emotionally charged moments on reality TV shows or in candid interviews, shedding light on their personal battles and sparking essential conversations about mental health.

This intersection of trauma and celebrity life weaves a compelling narrative that blurs the lines between reality and entertainment. The impacts of betrayal, infidelity, abuse, and childhood trauma reverberate not only in their personal lives but also in the broader cultural conversations about relationships, resilience, and relentlessly pursuing love. The world watches, captivated by a story that unfolds within the lenses of national television and other media, where the human experience is on display in all its raw and unfiltered glory.

CHAPTER TWENTY-ONE

The Trust Dilemma: Celebrities Battle for Authenticity

In the realm of famous love stories, trust is fragile, like a thin thread that can easily break. Think of it as a crucial character in a dramatic tale set against the backdrop of constant fame. But why does trust sometimes crumble, and how does it affect the complex love lives of celebrities?

Let's dive into the lives of our beloved stars. Often, their journey starts with scars from past betrayals, old wounds that haven't fully healed. Ex-partners who broke their trust and friends who became enemies are memories that haunt them.

These lingering doubts, the intense attention from the public, and the ever-watchful media create uncertainty about the intentions of those around them. The constant spotlight exposes every part of their lives, even the most innocent actions, leading to misunderstandings.

Another challenge they face is distance. Their careers demand constant travel, keeping them away from their loved ones for extended periods. This physical separation sometimes leads to emotional distance and insecurity.

In their world, safety is also a concern. Celebrities are aware that not everyone in their circle has good intentions. The constant spotlight can attract people who want to take advantage of or manipulate them, making trust even more complicated.

These trust issues often become the central problem in their relationships. Communication, which is essential for any relationship, suffers as celebrities fear sharing their thoughts due to the fear of betrayal. Jealousy often simmers beneath the surface, fueled by interactions with co-stars and colleagues. The need to prove their trustworthiness adds more pressure.

In some of the most heartbreaking moments, trust issues lead to self-sabotage. Driven by fear and convinced that pain is inevitable, celebrities push away partners who have done nothing wrong. These are the moments that test the strength of their love.

However, our celebrities remain resilient. They understand that trust, even in the glamorous world of fame, is the foundation of love. They navigate these challenges, knowing that trust is crucial even under the constant spotlight.

Their resolution is like the climax of a great story, requiring courage, vulnerability, and a deep exploration of the root causes. Trust, the cornerstone of their narrative, cannot be ignored. As they face these challenges, they discover that trust, even in the glittering world of fame, is the bedrock on which love is built. Through resilience, open communication, and understanding, their love story endures, proving that even under the harsh spotlight of fame, true love can triumph.

STRAIGHT from Safaree…

You know, trust and security in this celebrity world are a wild ride. It's like being in a constant maze, and sometimes that maze plays tricks on your mind. Trust issues are real, and they can mess with your head, especially when you're living in the spotlight.

But let me break it down for you with a real-life scenario, something I've seen up close and personal in this celebrity world. Trust and security are like the North Star in this maze of fame and attention.

Picture this: You're a celeb, constantly in the spotlight. You've got this amazing partner and everything's golden, or so you think. But then you're faced with a situation, a choice that tests that trust you've built.

Let's say you're at a star-studded event—cameras flashing, everyone watching. And there's this other celeb, charismatic, charming, and known for being a bit shady, especially regarding relationships. They start chatting up your partner, maybe a little too friendly for your comfort. The green-eyed monster, jealousy, starts creeping in. You start wondering, *What's going on there? Is it something more than just a chat?*

Now, here's where it gets tricky. You can't just jump to conclusions, but that doubt is like a relentless itch in your mind. Are they faithful? Is this just friendly banter or something deeper? Trust issues are like a storm brewing inside you.

And that's just one scenario. Trust and security are challenged in so many ways in this world. The physical distance when you're both chasing your dreams, the constant scrutiny by the media, the jealousy that sometimes rears its ugly head – it's a roller-coaster of emotions.

The fame itself is a double-edged sword, no doubt. On one side, you get love and adoration, but on the flip side, you get doubt and skepticism. You start second-guessing everyone's intentions. Are they here for you, or are they here for the glitz and the glam? It's like living with this constant cloud of insecurity hanging over you.

The physical distance doesn't help either. Celebs are always on the move, chasing their dreams, but that often means being away from the ones they care about. That physical distance can lead to emotional distance too, and that's where trust can start to crumble. You start wondering what's happening when you're not around, who they're with, and if they're staying true.

And then there's the relentless spotlight. Every little thing you do is under a microscope. A simple chat can turn into a headline in the media. This constant exposure can mess with your mind and make you hold back, afraid of how your actions might be twisted.

Jealousy is another beast. You see your partner mingling with other celebs, and that green-eyed monster rears its head. It's like a storm brewing inside you, and sometimes, that jealousy can make you act in ways you'll regret, pushing away people who genuinely care about you.

But here's the deal: Trust and security are like the foundation of any relationship, even in this glamorous world. You can't let past scars or the fear of what's ahead dictate your present. It's a journey, a tough one, but it's necessary.

Communication, my friend, is your lifeline. You've got to talk, be open, and yeah, be vulnerable. And as for choosing your partners, pick wisely. Surround yourself with people who get you, who support you. It's a process, an ongoing one, but it's worth it because trust and security are the rock on which love stands, even when the world is watching.

CHAPTER TWENTY-TWO

Privacy vs. Publicity: Navigating the Delicate Balance

The endless quest for celebrities to achieve perfection in their image, craft and relationships often leads to losing themselves in the public lives they portray. The immersive nature of their work can consume them, blurring the boundaries of their own identities and leaving a void where their true selves once lived. This entanglement of self and image can have a profound impact on their dating lives, shrouding potential relationships in a fog of uncertainty and disconnection.

When celebrities become engulfed in a role or even a public persona, they immerse themselves in the character's psyche, delving deep into their thoughts, emotions, and mannerisms. The process of character development becomes an all-encompassing journey, as they painstakingly research, internalize, and embody the essence of the person they are tasked to portray.

As the days turn into weeks and months on set, the lines between the actor and the character begin to blur. They may think, speak, and behave like the person they are playing, both on and off screen as well as in the media. The character's traits seep into their consciousness, becoming second nature, while their own personality and individuality take a backseat.

In this state of intense immersion, celebrities may experience a temporary loss of self-identity. They may find it challenging to distinguish between their own thoughts and those of the character they are embodying. The boundaries between their personal lives and the fictional world they inhabit become porous, leading to a blurring of their true selves and the personas they portray.

This transformation can infiltrate their daily lives, affecting their interactions with family, friends, and romantic partners. They may carry the remnants of the character's behaviors, speech patterns, and even beliefs into their personal relationships. Their loved ones may see a shift in their demeanor as they grapple with reconciling their true selves with the personas they inhabit.

In the realm of dating, the impact of this deep immersion can be profound. Celebrities may struggle to establish and maintain genuine connections as they oscillate between their own identities and those of the characters they portray. Potential partners may navigate a landscape of unpredictability, unsure of who they are engaging with.

The emotional toll of becoming so deeply entwined with a character can be immense. Celebrities may experience heightened levels of stress, emotional volatility, and internal conflicts as they navigate the complexities of their dual identities. This can create an emotional distance in their relationships, making it challenging to cultivate intimacy and trust with their partners.

The demands of their careers often require long hours on set, leaving little time for personal reflection and self-care. The relentless schedule, combined with the lingering remnants of their characters, can leave celebrities feeling mentally and physically drained. This exhaustion can spill over into their dating lives, resulting in a lack of energy and emotional availability for their partners.

In the midst of the challenges, there are those who find a delicate balance between their personal identities and the characters they portray. They learn to compartmentalize, letting their true selves shine through while embodying the essence of their characters when needed. These individuals are adept at switching on and off, seamlessly transitioning between the roles they play and their authentic selves. It is in these connections, based on mutual understanding and acceptance, that genuine relationships can flourish.

To maintain a sense of self and foster healthier connections, celebrities must focus on self-reflection and self-care. They need to create boundaries between their personal lives and the characters they portray, making sure their true identities remain intact. Seeking support from trusted mentors, therapists, and loved ones can provide a lifeline of guidance and reassurance as they navigate the complexities of their dual existence.

In the struggle to balance the demands of their craft and their personal lives, celebrities must confront the intricacies of losing themselves within the roles they play. It is a journey of self-discovery, resilience, and the unwavering commitment to remain true to oneself.

STRAIGHT from Safaree...

Yo, let me drop some real talk about this whole celeb life and staying true to yourself. Believe me, I've seen it all in this crazy world of fame and image. I've also had to battle with public perception and how to manage that privately.

First off, being authentic is like holding on to a tiny flame in a hurricane. When that spotlight hits you, it's showtime, right? Every move, every word—it's all under a microscope. You gotta play the game, wear the mask, and put on a show that the world wants to see.

But behind closed doors, when it's just you and your thoughts, that's when the real you shines brightly. It's definitely a battle, man, between the "you" the world wants and the "you" you truly are. And trust me, sometimes that battle gets exhausting.

See, the pressure to fit into this image of what a celeb should be is like a beast. You gotta watch how you talk, how you walk, what you eat, what you wear – it's all judged. And sometimes you lose sight of who you really are and what you want in all that noise.

The public loves and craves drama. Scandals, controversies— they eat that up. So you think, *Do I need to be perfect? Do I need to be this flawless image?* That's where things get messed up. You believe your own act.

But here's the thing: The real you, the flaws, the quirks—that's what makes you, you. That stuff connects you with real people.

So in those moments when you can be yourself, away from the paparazzi and the expectations, that's gold, man.

Dating? Oh, don't get me started. Imagine trying to date when everyone's got this preconceived idea of who you are. They see the headlines, the rumors, and they think they know you. It's like starting a race with a hundred-pound weight on your back.

And then there's the physical appearance standards. Yo, we all know how messed up that can be. The industry's got these insane expectations of how you have to look, dress and present yourself. You can't have one off day, and it can mess with your head. You're up one day, down the next, and it's like a rollercoaster for your self-esteem if you let it get to you.

But listen, there are real ones out there who see past the fame and the image nonsense. They get you for who you are, not for the persona you put out there. Those are the keepers, man. They help you find your way back to being authentic in times you may even question yourself. They can be like a mirror reflecting back the real you.

So what's the lesson here? Stay true to yourself, no matter how crazy life gets. Embrace your flaws, your quirks, and don't let the world's expectations suffocate your authenticity. And when you find someone who loves you for you, hold on tight, 'cause that's a rare gem in this wild ride of life. Peace!

CHAPTER TWENTY-THREE

Rebuilding Bridges: Balancing Family Life After a Celebrity Breakup

Balancing family life while dating a celebrity is a complex challenge, especially when that high-profile relationship ends publicly. It doesn't just affect the celebrity; their family also faces intense public scrutiny and judgment that can be overwhelming.

Think of it like this: Suddenly your family becomes the stars of a reality show, and the whole world is watching. Every little thing they do or say is magnified and analyzed. Simple outings or innocent interactions turn into gossip, and their personal lives become public entertainment.

The invasion of privacy doesn't stop at their doorstep; it infiltrates their homes, where privacy becomes a luxury they can't afford. Even their children can't escape the relentless media attention, growing up under a constant spotlight that shapes their self-esteem and identity.

This scrutiny extends to their professional lives as well. Colleagues and coworkers may treat them differently because of their celebrity connection, adding more stress to their already challenging situation.

For the family left behind after a public breakup, there's a void that can't be easily filled. The absence of the celebrity partner leaves a palpable emptiness in their lives. The shattered dreams and broken promises cast a long shadow, reminding them of what once was. There is a strong pull to speak on these emotions and give other opinions, but staying silent for the public prevents further scrutiny and helps everyone move on.

In this turmoil, the family must support one another and navigate the storm together. They become a lifeline for each other, offering comfort amidst the chaos. Solidarity and open communication are essential tools to help them cope with the challenges they face. Having a structured schedule and normalizing as many things as possible stabilize the situation too; having that new routine adds to the semblance of calm after the chaos.

Protecting the family from the constant onslaught of social media and public opinion becomes a battle they must fight relentlessly. Establishing boundaries and creating safe spaces for privacy are crucial. Sometimes taking a break from the online world can provide a much-needed respite from all the noise.

In this complex balance of family and celebrity life, celebrities and their families must prioritize self-care and emotional well-being. Seeking therapy or counseling can provide valuable support to help them navigate emotional complexities and cope with external pressures.

Balancing family and celebrity life after a public breakup is an ongoing process of adaptation and growth. It requires a deep commitment to maintaining healthy boundaries, nurturing strong familial bonds, and safeguarding the well-being of all involved. Through resilience, mutual support, and a shared determination to protect their loved ones, celebrities and their families can find a path forward amidst the challenges of fame and heartbreak.

STRAIGHT from Safaree...

Yo, peep this, fam: Imagine the straight-up chaos when a high-profile love story crashes and burns, and it isn't just the famous couple catching heat, but their whole fam too. It's like a full-on tornado of drama, emotions flying all over the place, and it's not just a personal matter anymore. Everybody in the vicinity gets sucked into this whirlwind of judgment and prying eyes.

Now, picture the family members of these celebs – regular folks suddenly thrust into this unforgiving spotlight. It's like their every move and every word is under a microscope, with the whole world watching. They lose their privacy, getting exposed and becoming vulnerable. Stuff that used to be chill, like going out or just being themselves, is now juicy gossip. Even their private relationships turn into a public spectacle.

And this never-ending scrutiny even messes with their homes, where they can't get a moment's peace. The media circus barges right in, like they have no boundaries. Think about the kids in these families, growing up in a world where every tiny mistake or innocent thing they do gets blown way out of proportion. The weight of what the public thinks messes with their heads, messing up their self-esteem and self-image.

Even when these family members do their own thing, they can't escape the spotlight. People see them through the celeb connection, laying down unfair judgments and unwanted attention. The pressure to fit into some image or to distance themselves from the breakup mess is just too much. It piles on the stress, making their lives even crazier.

And don't forget about the family left behind after a super public breakup – there's a gap, a hole that can't be filled. Without the famous partner, a noticeable emptiness messes with everything. Dreams and promises are crushed, and the pain hangs around like a ghost.

But in all this madness, the family's gotta stick together, hold it down, and weather the storm side by side. They become each other's support, like a safe haven in all the craziness. They need that unity and honest conversations to stay sane, finding comfort in sharing their experiences and creating a spot where they can be themselves, flaws and all.

Now, protecting the fam from the constant social media drama and public opinions is a real battle. They gotta set boundaries and carve out spaces where they can keep their privacy. Sometimes they just gotta unplug from the online world, even if it's just for a bit, to escape all the opinions and judgments.

In this tricky dance of balancing family life and the celeb circus, it's crucial for both the famous folks and their fam to look out for themselves, mentally and emotionally. Getting some therapy or counseling can help them handle all the emotions, process their feelings, and deal with all the outside pressures.

Keeping that balance between family and celeb life after a mega-public breakup is all about adapting and growing. It's like a commitment to keep healthy boundaries, nurture strong family bonds, and protect everyone's well-being. They gotta be strong, support each other, and stay determined to keep their loved ones safe in the middle of all this celeb madness. Peace!

CHAPTER TWENTY-FOUR

Celebrity Dating Takeaways

The lessons we learn from the world of celebrity dating are crystal clear. They offer valuable insights into the dynamic interplay of love and fame, highlighting both the highs and lows of this unique journey.

In its most enchanting moments, celebrity dating shows the resilience of love, transcending societal boundaries even amid the dazzling chaos of red-carpet events and movie premieres. It stands as a testament to the boundless nature of affection, reminding us it is not constrained by the trappings of fame.

However, beneath the glittering surface lies a darker narrative. The weight of relentless media scrutiny can turn relationships into battlegrounds, eroding the sanctity of privacy and authenticity. Rumors and gossip, like wildfire, can engulf even the most robust connections, underscoring that love, even in the limelight, grapples with challenges like those of ordinary relationships.

Amidst the allure of extravagant escapades to far-flung destinations and indulgent shopping sprees, a cautionary tale unfolds.

The temptations of opulence and excess can inadvertently cultivate a culture of materialism and superficiality, where authentic connections become ensnared in a web of material desires, serving as a stark reminder that true love cannot be acquired through material possessions.

The media, a double-edged sword, wields its influence both positively and negatively. Positive media coverage celebrates love stories, offering a beacon of hope amidst fame's chaos. However, the dark side reveals itself through invasive intrusions and the propagation of hurtful rumors. The media's impact can poison minds and corrode relationships, leaving enduring scars in its wake.

In navigating the labyrinthine terrain of celebrity dating, these lessons guide us. They emphasize the significance of discernment, encouraging us to value authenticity and shared values above the allure of fame and excess. They prompt us to nurture trust amidst the tempest of media scrutiny and to treasure genuine connections that surpass the superficial.

The lessons drawn from celebrity dating underline the intricacies inherent in the intersection of love and fame. They call upon us to approach relationships with wisdom, empathy, and a commitment to our emotional well-being. By heeding these lessons, we can navigate the labyrinth of love, fame, and its attendant chaos, forging our own paths amid the unpredictable currents of the celebrity dating world.

In summary, the mosaic of celebrity dating intricately weaves tales of love, betrayal, and resilience. It urges us to embrace the beauty of genuine connections while remaining vigilant against the erosive forces that fame can unleash. Let us glean wisdom from the positive and negative facets of this world as we chart our own romantic voyages, guided by the insights derived from love's intricate dance in the public eye.

STRAIGHT from Safaree...

Yo, what's good, everyone? It's your boy Safaree, and we've dived deep into the lessons you learn when you're in the game of celebrity dating. Trust me, it's a wild ride, and I've offered the inside scoop for you.

First off, love is a powerful thing, and it doesn't care if you're walking down the red carpet or kicking it at home. Love transcends all that fame stuff, and it's a beautiful reminder that we're all human underneath it all.

But here's the deal: When you're in the spotlight, it's like every move you make is up for public debate. The media can turn your relationship into a full-blown drama. They'll gossip, spread rumors, and invade your privacy like there's no tomorrow. It's a constant battle to keep your love strong amidst all that noise.

Then there's the flashy stuff – those luxury trips, designer shopping sprees, and all that jazz. But material things can't replace a genuine connection. It's the real love, the deep connection, that's worth more than any fancy car or expensive vacation.

The media is a double-edged sword. Positive coverage can be a breath of fresh air, giving you hope and celebrating your love. But when they start digging into your personal life or spreading lies, it's like dealing with a toxic relationship you can't escape.

So what's the takeaway here, folks? Stay true to yourself. Fame might change material things, but it can't change who you are at the core. Find someone who loves you for you, not the celebrity persona. Keep it real, value trust, and nurture those genuine connections.

Celebrity dating teaches us that love and fame can be a crazy mix, but we've got what it takes to navigate it. Stay authentic, stay grounded, and keep that love burning bright.

Conclusion

Thank you for joining us on this amazing journey, where we've explored *The World of Celebrity Dating: Unveiling the Truth behind the Glamour*. As we conclude this adventure, let's take a moment to reflect on what we've learned about celebrity relationships.

Throughout our exploration, we've gone beyond the glamorous facade of celebrity love stories and delved into the complexities that famous couples face. We've seen that being in the public eye isn't always easy; it comes with its own challenges. But we've also seen how love can conquer even the toughest obstacles.

By focusing on celebrities, we've gained insights into their world and the unique dynamics they navigate. These stories have given us a deeper understanding of the ups and downs of love when you're in the spotlight. They remind us that celebrities, like everyone else, experience the highs and lows of relationships.

As we wrap this up, I encourage you to take away these valuable lessons from the realm of celebrity dating. May you approach their world with a more discerning eye, recognizing the humanity behind the fame. Understanding the realities of celebrity romance can help us appreciate the complexities of love in all its forms.

I want to express my gratitude for being a part of this enlightening journey. As we bid farewell, remember to keep exploring the world of celebrity dating, for it offers a unique window into the intricate tapestry of love and fame.

Safe travels on your continuing journey, and may you find inspiration and insight in the world of celebrity romance.

STRAIGHT from Safaree...
Closing Remarks

I appreciate you going on this wild ride and digging deeper into a world that I've been living and experiencing in my quest for love. We're about to wrap this journey up now that we've peeled back some layers and given you a taste. You now know what you see isn't always what you're getting and everything is way more complex when looking for love as a celebrity. But before we drop the final curtain, let's take a moment to see all that we covered.

The allure of celebrity dating is like holding that elusive golden ticket to a world of pure fantasy. We looked at it all – red carpets, extravagant gifts, globetrotting adventures – the stuff dreams are made of. But we also saw the real deal of the pressure, the pain and the challenges. Still, who wouldn't want a taste of that good life, right?

But you know what's even more intriguing? It's what lies beneath the surface. Celebrities share a unique unspoken bond, one forged in the fires of fame. We've ridden the rollercoaster of stardom, experienced the dazzling highs, and weathered the stormy lows. So as for finding love together, it's more than just a connection; it's like finding someone who speaks the same cryptic language.

Of course, we can't ignore the challenges. Privacy? That's about as rare as a unicorn in this world. Media frenzy? Trust me, it's a daily occurrence for me. And the relentless pursuit of perfection some feel? It's enough to make your head spin faster than a record.

But in all this madness, I must believe that love can endure. When it's built on trust, respect, and shared values, it becomes an unbreakable anchor in the storm. There are celebrity couples out there who've shown us that love can shine its brightest even in the craziest of spotlights.

Going on this journey has been like riding the wildest roller-coaster at the fanciest theme park. It's made us reflect on our own love stories, leading us to question what matters in relationships. And it has reminded us that underneath the glitz and glamour, celebrities are just regular people searching for genuine connections.

So as we bring this adventure to a close, remember that the allure of celebrity dating mirrors the everyday thirst for connection, adventure, and a dash of the extraordinary. It's been a trip, and I wouldn't change a thing.

It's time for me to sign off, hoping your love story becomes legendary.

Stay blessed!

Love

"In love, you have to be willing to accept imperfections and work through challenges together." - Idris Elba

"Love isn't just about how someone makes you feel, but about who they help you become." - Oprah Winfrey

"Love takes off masks that we fear we cannot live without and know we cannot live within." - James Baldwin

"If you want to fly, you have to give up the things that weigh you down." - Toni Morrison

"In love, humble yourself, be open to life, and let the journey take you wherever it leads." - Janelle Monáe

"Love is a collaboration, and dating is the process of creating a masterpiece together." - John Legend

Dating is the rehearsal for a lifelong performance of love; make each practice count." - Regina King

"Relationships are like mirrors; they reflect back the aspects of yourself that need attention and growth." - Viola Davis

"A strong relationship starts with two people who are ready to stand together and face anything that comes their way." - Beyoncé

"In love, laughter is the secret ingredient that keeps the connection strong and the bond unbreakable." - Issa Rae

"Love is an ongoing dialogue; it's about listening, understanding, and responding with care." - Chadwick Boseman

"Once we realize nothing is more important than our happiness and peace of mind, we will do anything to protect our emotions and energy from being drained." - Clarence KD McNair

"In relationships, it's important to approach challenges with a champion's mindset—perseverance, resilience, and unwavering support." - Serena Williams

"Dating is like comedy; it's all about timing, chemistry, and finding someone who laughs at your jokes." - Kevin Hart

"A successful relationship is a collaboration, where two individuals inspire and elevate each other to reach new heights." - Kendrick Lamar

Meet *co-author Jason Gathing*, a luminary in personal transformation, renowned for his groundbreaking book "The Launch Code Unleashed." With a master's degree in education and specialized training in behavior analysis, Jason excels at the intersection of behavior, mindset, and holistic well-being. His inspiring mission is to help individuals make profound, positive changes in their lives by breaking free from self-limiting patterns, offering invaluable insights into human behavior, cognitive processes, and emotional well-being. As a Habit Specialist, his revolutionary approach combines behavioral science, psychology, and personal development to empower individuals to unlock their full potential, equipping them with practical tools and personalized strategies to conquer life's challenges. Under Jason's guidance, clients embark on a transformative journey to realize their deepest dreams, shedding self-limiting beliefs, and becoming architects of their destinies. With his expertise, dreams become reality, and personal and professional growth reaches extraordinary heights.

www.ingramcontent.com/pod-product-compliance
Lightning Source LLC
Chambersburg PA
CBHW070757300326
41914CB00053B/696